50 WALKS IN

Derbyshire

50 WALKS OF 2–10 MILES

First published 2001
New edition 2008
Reprinted July 2009, February and July 2010

Researched and written by John Gillham
Field checked and updated 2008 by Andrew McCloy

Series Management: Bookwork Creative Associates
Series Editors: Sandy Draper and Marilynne Lanng
Series Design Concept: Elizabeth Baldin and Andrew Milne
Picture Research: Alice Earle
Proofreader: Pamela Stagg
Cartography provided by the Mapping Services Department of AA Publishing

Produced by AA Publishing

Published by AA Publishing (a trading name of AA Media Limited, whose registered office is Fanum House, Basing View, Basingstoke, Hampshire RG21 4EA; registered number 06112600)

A04520

ISBN: 978-0-7495-6048-5
ISBN: 978-0-7495-6386-8 (SS)

A CIP catalogue record for this book is available from the British Library.

Visit AA Publishing at theAA.com/shop

Colour reproduction by Keenes Group, Andover
Printed by Printer Trento Srl, Italy

Acknowledgements
The Automobile Association would like to thank the following photographers, companies and picture libraries for their assistance in the preparation of this book.

Photography by Tom Mackie with the exception of p102 by A J Hopkins

Illustrations by Andrew Hutchinson

Every effort has been made to trace the copyright holders, and we apologise in advance for any accidental errors. We would be happy to apply the corrections in the following edition of this publication.

Right: Dove Dale, Peak District National Park (Walks 43 & 44)

AA

50 WALKS IN

Derbyshire

50 WALKS OF 2–10 MILES

50 WALKS

Contents

Contents

Rating

Each walk is rated for its relative difficulty compared to the other walks in this book. Walks marked +++ are likely to be shorter and easier with little total ascent. The hardest walks are marked +++

Walking in Safety

For advice and safety tips see page 144.

Locator Map

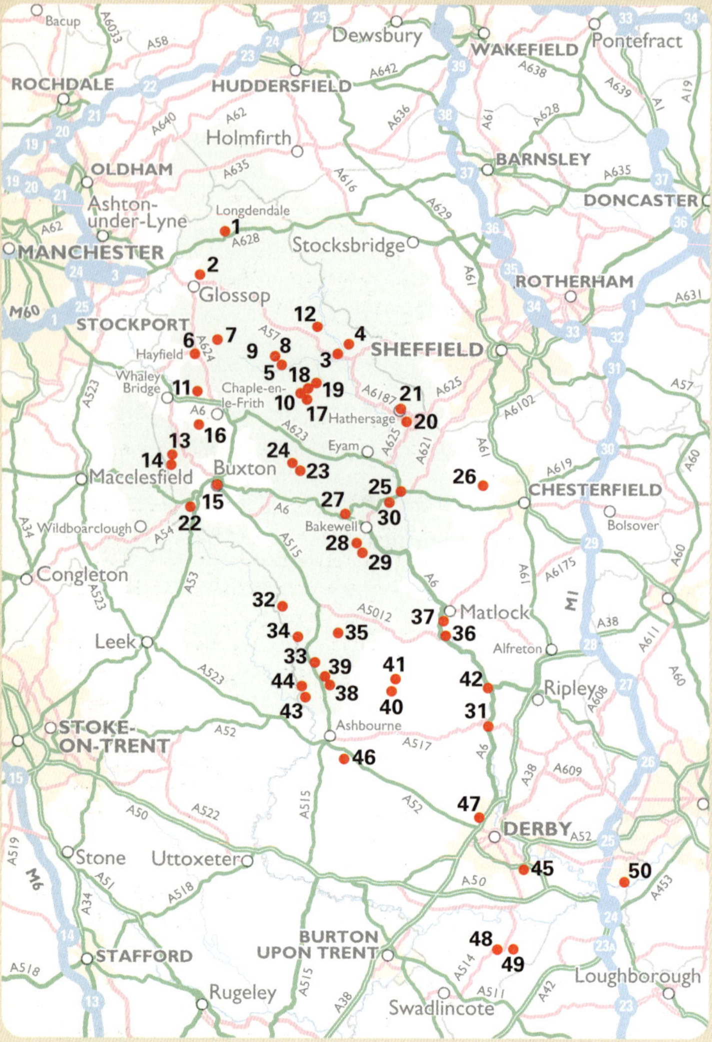

Legend

	Walk Route		Built-up Area
	Route Waypoint		Woodland Area
	Adjoining Path		Toilet
	Viewpoint		Car Park
	Place of Interest		Picnic Area
	Steep Section		Bridge

Introducing Derbyshire

Derbyshire: well that's the Peak District with Derby and the bit to the south isn't it? In reality however, Derbyshire spreads its borders a little wider than you may think. Here the brooding Pennine hills of the North meet the soft green plains of the South, but the change happens slowly, subtly; and in fascinating geological fashion. And much of the county's beautiful countryside lies outside Britain's first and most popular national park.

The county has four distinct regions: the Dark Peak, upland country formed by the silt from great rivers; the White Peak, an underlying layer of limestone formed when Derbyshire was under a tropical sea; the North East Derbyshire coalfields, and the clay and sandstone plains of the Trent. It's these contrasts of landscape that makes Derbyshire such a fine place for either a mammoth mountain walk or just a stroll through the woods.

Dark to White

Many walkers are introduced to the Dark Peak when undertaking the Pennine Way, which begins at Edale and straddles the high moors of Kinder Scout, Bleaklow and Black Hill before heading north to the Scottish Borders. It's a good way to start, but your impressions will be more of the bone-crunching slabs that have been laid along the path than of the scenery. The best walks in the Dark Peak take you to the remote places, where you'll see the gritstone sculptures of devils and anvils, where the heather still clings to the rocks and where the pretty white flowers of the cloudberry peep through the moor grasses and peat.

The transition to the White Peak happens at Castleton. Here, the gritstone and crumbling shales of Mam Tor and the Great Ridge have been worn down to reveal the limestone. At Castleton you enter a world of gleaming tiered cliffs, caves and underground streams, deep wooded gorges (dales), and of high pastures captured by an intricate web of dry-stone walling. The dales: Dovedale, Lathkill Dale, Monsal Dale and Wolfscote Dale, have sent generations of writers and poets, including Wordsworth, Tennyson and Ruskin into raptures of purple prose.

A Grand Scenery

So what of the scenery outside the Peak District National Park? Well, there's plenty of it to choose from. There is Matlock Bath, a mini Blackpool, shoehorned into the narrow defile of the Derwent Gorge. A few hundred yards after leaving the Bedlam of its bright lights and amusement parlours, striding through woodland or crossing flower-filled meadows – a few hundred more and you can be high on the hillsides, looking across half of the county.

You cannot write a book of Derbyshire walks without including Derby. In recent years the authorities have reclaimed much of the railway land by the Derwent, making possible a fascinating riverside journey from the outskirts of the city to its cathedral.

The coalmines which once surrounded Chesterfield have been

PUBLIC TRANSPORT

Although there is reasonably good rail access to Edale and the Hope Valley from Sheffield and Manchester, regular public transport isn't one of the county's strongpoints. In the remoter areas you can wait for a bus for a couple of days! None of the walks described therefore relies on public transport, and the linear ones are mostly 'there-and-back' walks. For details of public transport, ring the national enquiry line on 0870 608 2 608 between 7am and 8pm, or look on the internet (www.pti.org.uk).

flattened and returned to nature. It is a strange experience walking through newly planted woodland and pastures that once would have reverberated to the sound of pit machinery and the rumblings of long trains loaded with soot-stained coal trucks. But it's all part of a regeneration process and the wildlife that was absent for a century is now returning to the region.

The county has more than its fair share of magnificent historical buildings. Chatsworth House is considered by many to be Britain's finest mansions, but it is only one of many. In this book we also visit Calke Abbey and Melbourne Hall and look across to Keddleston Hall.

So that is Derbyshire: all you have to do now is to get your boots on, get out there and start walking.

Using this book

INFORMATION PANELS

An information panel for each walk shows its relative difficulty (see page 5), the distance and total amount of ascent. An indication of the gradients you will encounter is shown by the rating ▲▲▲ (no steep slopes) to ▲▲▲ (several very steep slopes).

MAPS

There are 30 maps, covering 40 of the walks. Some walks have a suggested option in the same area. The information panel for these walks will tell you how much extra walking is involved. On short-cut suggestions the panel will tell you the total distance if you set out from the start of the main walk. Where an option returns to the same point on the main walk, just the distance of the loop is given. Where an option leaves the main walk at one point and returns to it at another, then the distance shown is for the whole walk. The minimum time suggested is for reasonably fit walkers and doesn't allow for stops. Each walk has a suggested map.

START POINTS

The start of each walk is given as a six-figure grid reference prefixed by two letters indicating which 100km square of the National Grid it refers to. You'll find more information on grid references on most Ordnance Survey maps.

DOGS

We have tried to give dog owners useful advice about how dog friendly each walk is. Please respect other countryside users. Keep your dog under control, especially around livestock, and obey local bylaws and other dog control notices.

CAR PARKING

Many of the car parks suggested are public, but occasionally you may find you have to park on the roadside or in a lay-by. Please be considerate when you leave your car, ensuring that access roads or gates are not blocked and that other vehicles can pass safely.

Right: Mam Tor to Hollins Cross, Peak District National Park (Walk 17)

Manchester's Bit of Derbyshire

In Longdendale, the wild Pennines meet the bustling metropolis.

DISTANCE *7.5 miles (12.1km)* **MINIMUM TIME** *4hrs*

ASCENT/GRADIENT *1,180ft (360m)* ▲▲▲ **LEVEL OF DIFFICULTY** +++

PATHS *Good paths and tracks, a few stiles*

LANDSCAPE *Heather moorland, and rolling farm pastures*

SUGGESTED MAP *OS Explorer OL1 Dark Peak*

START/FINISH *Grid reference: SK 073994*

DOG FRIENDLINESS *Walk is on farmland and access agreement land, dogs should be kept on lead*

PARKING *Crowden pay car park*

PUBLIC TOILETS *At car park and Torside car park*

Longdendale, the valley of the River Etherow, threads deep into the Pennines between the craggy cliffs of Bleaklow and the sullen slopes of Black Hill. In bygone centuries this must have been an inhospitable but dramatic wilderness of heath and bog.

Meanwhile in nearby Manchester, the Industrial Revolution had caused a dramatic increase in the population from around 10,000 to over 230,000. This meant that Manchester needed more water, and its engineers turned to Longdendale. Between 1848 and 1877 a string of five reservoirs were built to the designs of John Frederic La Trobe Bateman. Later came the railway, linking Manchester with Sheffield, then came electricity. So this remote narrow valley was filled with the contraptions of the modern world. Manchester's people came here in their thousands, using the railway and taking to the hills.

Pennine Wayfarers

Crowden is one of the few settlements in the valley. Around the youth hostel you'll often see weary walkers, weighed down with heavy backpacks. More often than not they will have just completed the first day of the Pennine Way over Kinder Scout and Bleaklow. In the book they're clutching Alfred Wainwright has told them how unsightly Longdendale is, and how they will continue towards the horrors of Black Hill's bogs.

But this walk shows you the very best of Longdendale. The railway has gone now, dismantled in 1981 with the decline of the coal industry. After strolling down to the Torside Reservoir you follow its trackbed, now part of the Longdendale Trail. Soon you've left the valley behind and you're climbing through the shade of woods, where oak, birch, larch and pine are mixed with open patches of heather and bilberry. Longdendale looks pretty good now. Bleaklow's ruffled peat-hagged top is fronted by a bold line of cliffs, which overlook the valley's blue lakes and emerald fields. Several streams plummet down shady ravines, while Torside Clough, a huge gash in the side of the fell, dwarfs the little farm at its foot.

Now you're on the moors with squat cliffs of Millstone Rocks lying across cotton grass moors. At Lad's Leap, the Hollins Clough stream tumbles over a slabbed rocky bed into Coombes Clough. Who knows who the lad was that could leap across this gap, but he must have had long legs, or a good imagination.

Mere mortals descend to ford the stream before continuing above Highstone Rocks to the rim of the Crowden valley where you can look deep into the inner recesses of Black Hill. Below, just a short descent away, your car awaits back at Crowden.

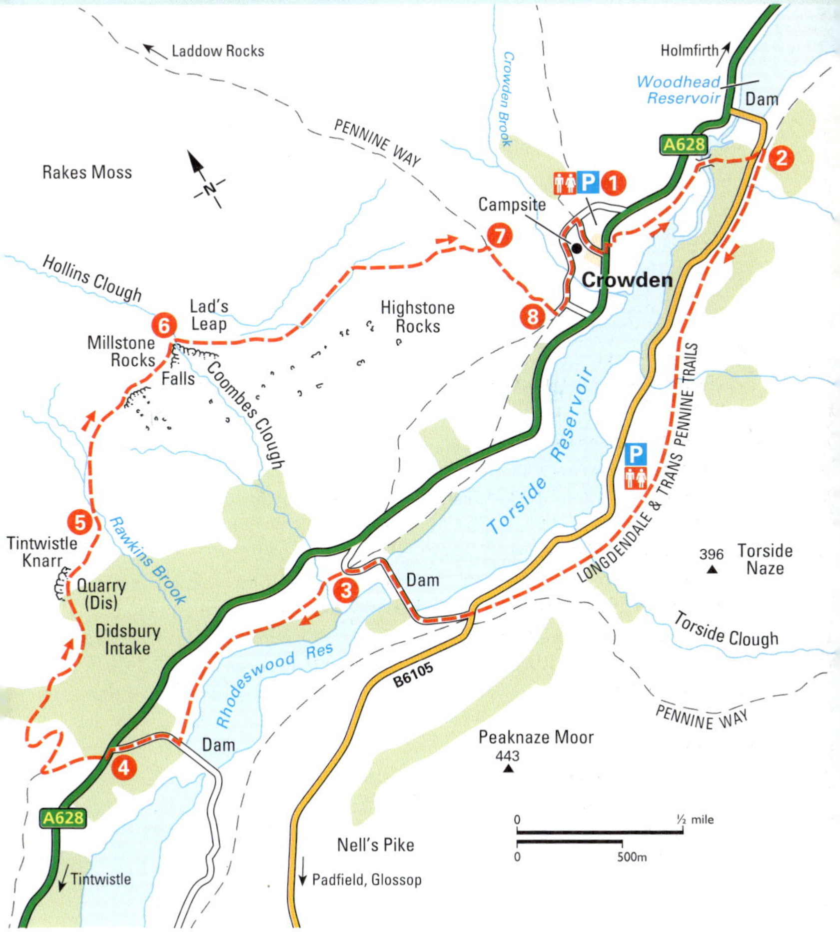

WALK 1 DIRECTIONS

1 Leave the car park and cross the A628. Take the permissive footpath east before crossing a footbridge over the Etherow beneath the Woodhead dam. Passing through a small wood, the path meets a road. Cross it to join the Longdendale and Trans Pennine Trails.

2 Turn right along the trackbed, following the two trails westwards above the south shore of Torside Reservoir. Leave the track where it crosses the road, then follow the lane opposite, crossing the dam to the north shore. At the apex of a right-hand bend leave the lane for another permissive footpath, this time heading west above Rhodeswood Reservoir.

3 After going through the left of two gates, follow the path through some scrub woodland to reach the Rhodeswood dam, where a tarmac lane takes you back to the main road.

WHERE TO EAT AND DRINK

Hot and cold drinks, ice creams and confectionary are available from the campsite shop at Crowden (open to the public in season). For pub meals, visit the Peels Arms on Temple Street, Padfield (off Glossop Road). It is a traditional village pub, serving decent ale and good food daily.

4 Turn left along the road for a few paces, then cross it to climb on a track right of the intake wall. Turn right to follow an old quarry track that zig-zags up heather and grass slopes before delving into the woods of Didsbury Intake. The track passes between the cliffs and the bouldery landslip area of Tintwistle Knarr Quarry.

5 After leaving the woods behind you reach the brim of the moor by Rawkins Brook. Go over the stile in the fence and trace a peaty path known as Black Gutter. This heads roughly north-east across heathland towards the gritstone 'edge' of Millstone Rocks.

WHILE YOU'RE THERE

It's worth doing a short there-and-back walk along the Pennine Way to see Laddow Rocks. The fine tiered gritstone cliffs, which lie in the heart of the Crowden valley, were popular with climbers in the early 1900s. Today, most of the climbers have moved on to the more challenging (and accessible) eastern edges, such as Stanage, Curbar and Froggat.

6 Follow the edge to Lad's Leap, where you descend to ford the Hollins Clough stream before climbing back on to the moors. A dilapidated wall comes in from the right, and the path descends with it into the Crowden valley.

7 Half-way down the slope it meets the Pennine Way route, where you turn right, descending towards Torside Reservoir.

8 Turn left to walk along a prominent unsurfaced lane that descends parallel to the northern shore of the reservoir and then continues to the bottom of the Crowden valley. Walk across the bridge over Crowden Brook and then follow the walled lane as it curves right to reach a crossroads. Turn right, passing the campsite and toilet block, to return to the car park.

WHAT TO LOOK OUT FOR

The Longdendale Trail was the trackbed for the Great Central Railway's Woodhead line, built in 1847 to link Manchester and Sheffield. The line, which included the 3-mile (4.8km) Woodhead Tunnel through the Pennine ridge, claimed many lives – 32 for the tunnel alone. Those who died in the hostile damp conditions are unrecorded, but 28 workers perished in a cholera epidemic of 1849. Some of the graves can be seen at Woodhead Chapel, just off-route above the Woodhead Reservoir's dam.

Avoiding the Black Stuff

There is more to the peatlands of Bleaklow than mile upon mile of bog.

DISTANCE *7 miles (11.3km)* **MINIMUM TIME** *4hrs*

ASCENT/GRADIENT *1,500ft (460m)* ▲▲▲ **LEVEL OF DIFFICULTY** +++

PATHS *Unsurfaced tracks and moorland paths, a few stiles*

LANDSCAPE *High peat moor*

SUGGESTED MAP *OS Explorer OL1 Dark Peak*

START/FINISH *Grid reference: SK 043947*

DOG FRIENDLINESS *Access agreement land, dogs should be kept on lead*

PARKING *Manor Park car park, off Glossop High Street East (A57)*

PUBLIC TOILETS *At car park*

Bleaklow's not so much a hill, more a vast expanse of bare black peat, where even the toughest moor grasses can't take root. Wainwright once wrote that nobody loved the place, and those who got on it were glad to get off. But there's another side to Bleaklow. There are corners where bilberries grow thick round fascinating rock sculptures; where heather, bracken and grass weave a colourful quilt draped beneath wide skies. Places like Grinah Stones, Yellowslacks and Shepherd's Meeting Stones are all remote, but they're dramatic places, far superior to anything seen on the popular routes. Bleaklow's true top lies in the midst of the mires, but only a few feet lower is Higher Shelf Stones, a bold summit with a distinctive mountain shape – and some good crags. Climb Higher Shelf Stones from Old Glossop, and you'll see the best of Bleaklow.

Old Glossop

Time has been kind to Old Glossop. Planners and industrialists of the 19th and 20th centuries built their shops and factories further west, leaving the old quarter untouched. Here 17th-century cottages of darkened gritstone line cobbled streets, overlooked by the spired All Saints Church. Shepley Street takes you into the hills, and it's not long before you're climbing the heathery spur of Lightside and looking across the rocky ravine of Yellowslacks. A fine path develops on the cliffedge before entering the confines of Dowstone Clough, which clambers towards Higher Shelf Stones. Eventually the clough shallows and the stream becomes a trickle in the peat, leaving you to find your own way. Sandy channels, known as groughs, lead you southwards.

Higher Shelf Stones

Suddenly, the peat ends and the trig point appears. From the summit rocks you look down on the deep twisting clough of Shelf Brook and out across the plains of Manchester to the shadowy hills of North Wales. It's time to leave the high moors. There's a faint path across a grassy spur descending into Shelf Brook's clough, where you join the Doctor's Gate track. This gets its name from John Talbot, the Vicar of Glossop 1450–94, who often used the road to visit his father in Sheffield. His trips were worthy of note because he was in fact the illegitimate son of the very powerful Earl of Shrewsbury. Much earlier, the old highway was used by Roman troops marching between their forts at Navio (Brough, near Hope) and Melandra (Glossop). We follow their footsteps as the paved track twists through the clough, by the rounded Shire Hill and back to Old Glossop.

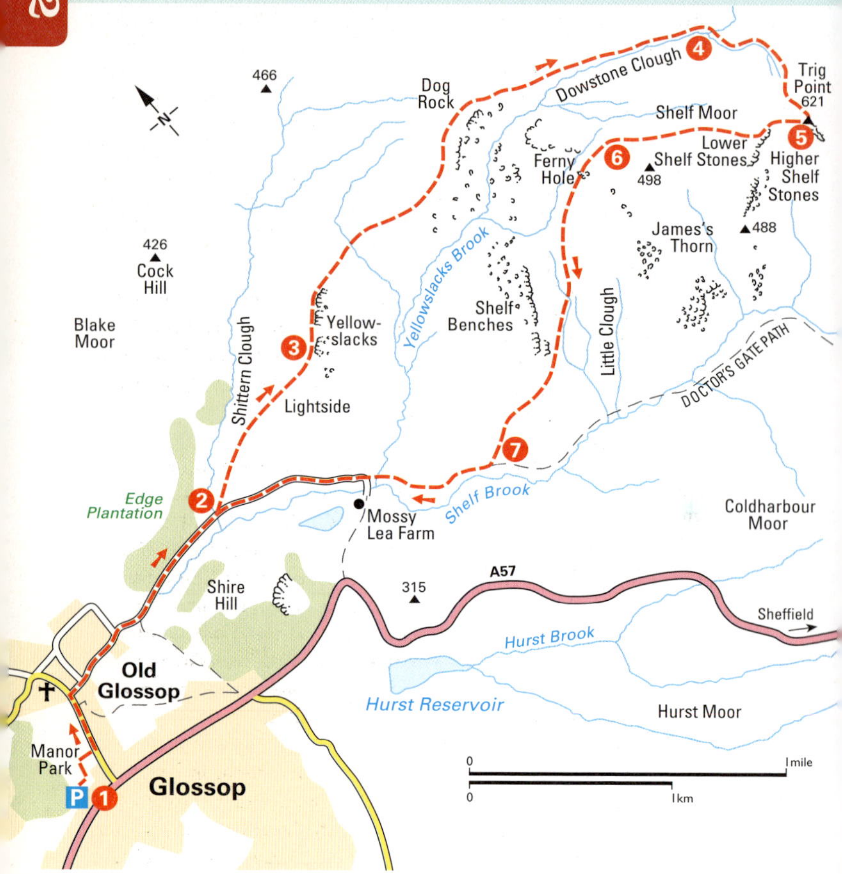

WALK 2 DIRECTIONS

1 From the car park, walk through Manor Park and then turn left along Manor Park Road into Old Glossop. Turn right along Shepley Street, passing the factory to the bus turning circle. Here a farm track continues eastwards, with the partially wooded dome of Shire Hill on the right and the pine- and oak-clad slopes of Edge Plantation on the left.

2 Leave the track at a ladder stile. Cross the stile on to a path, confined at first by a fence and dry-stone wall, that climbs north-east on a pastured spur overlooking the curiously named but pleasant craggy valley of Shittern Clough. In the upper reaches and beyond a second ladder stile, the now well-defined path continues the climb through bilberry bushes and then over the heather of Upper Lightside.

3 A narrow path switches to the spur's southern brow high above Yellowslacks Brook. A dilapidated wire fence comes in from the right and the path goes along the right-hand side of it before joining the cliff edges of Yellowslacks and Dog Rock. The crags close in to form the rugged channel of Dowstone Clough. The path, now intermittent, stays close to the stream and keeps away from the peat hags.

WHILE YOU'RE THERE

Glossop is a fascinating, bustling town to visit. It's known locally as Howard's Town in tribute to its 19th-century benefactors. Bernard Edward Howard, the 12th Duke of Norfolk, was one of the founders of the first cotton mills in the area. By 1831 there were 30 in the town. At this time the grand town hall, the Square and the Roman Catholic church were built. You can find out more about the town and it's history at the Heritage Centre in Henry Street.

4 As the clough shallows and the stream divides among a bed of rushes (grid ref 089954), aim for Higher Shelf Stones by crossing the main stream and following its southbound tributary – just follow the bootprints along its sandy bed, which snakes through a complex of peat hags in a southbound direction. Near the summit of Higher Shelf Stones the channel shallows and widens then, suddenly, the trig point rises from a grassy plinth ahead.

5 From Higher Shelf Stones, trace the brow of Shelf Moor towards Lower Shelf Stones then on to James's Thorn, on a narrow path, but circumvent the naked peat that proliferates on the left. A prominent grassy channel descends just north of west and forms a reliable and reasonably dry course down over Shelf Moor to a boulder-strewn edge above Ferny Hole.

WHAT TO LOOK OUT FOR

East of the summit of Higher Shelf Stones look for the remains of a US Air Force Superfortress bomber, which crashed here in 1948 killing its crew. Walkers have reported seeing ghosts near the site. From here you can detour round the edge of the clough to the rock outcrops on James's Thorn, where there's another plane wreck.

A small monument with a pile of wreckage marks the place where, on 18 May 1945, a Canadian Lancaster bomber crashed.

6 From here down to the Doctor's Gate path, soon visible far below, follow a faint but discernible path that weaves its way down the rough hillside east of Shelf Benches. Towards the bottom, it merges with a wider, grassy track and joins Doctor's Gate by a stone barn. Continue down the valley.

7 Doctor's Gate meanders through the moorland clough of Shelf Brook before passing Mossy Lea Farm. Continue straight on to join the outward route at the foot of Lightside, which brings you back to Old Glossop.

WHERE TO EAT AND DRINK

The small café in Manor Park sells ice creams and snacks throughout the summer season. For more substantial fare, visit The Queens on Shepley Street in Old Glossop, which serves a good selection of bar and restaurant meals daily, plus a range of real ales and coffees.

WALK 3

A High Ridge and Lost Villages at Ladybower

Beneath the beauty of the Ladybower Reservoir lie the remains of the old village of Ashopton.

DISTANCE *5.5 miles (8.8km)* **MINIMUM TIME** *3hrs 30min*

ASCENT/GRADIENT *1,200ft (365m)* ▲▲▲ **LEVEL OF DIFFICULTY** +++

PATHS *Well-defined moorland paths and a reservoir road*

LANDSCAPE *High gritstone moorland*

SUGGESTED MAP *Explorer OL1 Dark Peak*

START/FINISH *Grid reference: SK 195864*

DOG FRIENDLINESS *Keep on lead on access agreement land, could run free by reservoir shores*

PARKING *Marked roadside parking bay east of Ashopton Viaduct*

PUBLIC TOILETS *Heatherdene car park (off A6013) and Fairholmes*

In the north-east corner of Derbyshire, the heather ridges and gritstone tors of Derwent Edge make one last stand before declining to the plains of Yorkshire. It's always been a sparsely populated corner of the country with few references in the history books. Hereabouts, the stories lie beneath the water.

Before the Second World War Ashopton, which lay at the confluence of the rivers Derwent and Ashop, was a huddle of stone-built cottages, a small inn and a blacksmith's shop. A little lane ambled from Ashopton northwards to its neighbouring village, Derwent, which enjoyed an even quieter location in the Upper Derwent valley. But the building of a huge reservoir, the third in the region, shattered the locals' lives. After the completion of its dam in 1943 Ladybower Reservoir gradually filled up, and by 1946 the water level had risen above the rooftops.

Haunting Remains

Wherever you look there is water. From the banks of Ladybower Reservoir, on the east side of the huge concrete viaduct, you take a winding track up the hill, now shaded by a sombre plantation of spruce. The cottages you see here are all that remain of the village of Ashopston.

Soon you're through the woods and heading across open moor to the weathered gritstone tors that top the ridge. The rocks of Whinstone Lee Tor are set into a thick carpet of heather. Though the highest hills in the region lie to the north, this is one of the best viewpoints, as the ridge is at its narrowest here. In the west, Kinder Scout's expansive flat top peeps over Crook Hill's rocky crest. In the valley below the dark waters of the reservoir still keep their secrets.

After passing the Hurkling Stones, the route descends towards the waterside in search of Derwent village. The old gateposts of Derwent Hall still survive by the roadside. A notice board shows the positions of the hall itself, along with the post office, school, church and some of the old cottages. After a dry spell the water level can sometimes fall sufficiently for you to see the crumbling walls and foundations of the village surrounded by the crazed drying mud. One small bridge is almost intact, but the villagers dismantled the main twin-arched packhorse bridge for rebuilding beyond the reach of the rising water at Slippery Stones, higher up the valley.

Leaving the old village behind you return by the shores of the reservoir. Nature has readjusted. The landscape, though more regimented now, is still beautiful; kestrels still scour the hillside for prey, and dippers frequent the streams as they always have done.

WALK 3 DIRECTIONS

1 On the east side of Ashopton Viaduct, take the private road (a public footpath) that zig-zags up past a few of Ashopton's remaining cottages.

2 The road becomes unsurfaced and gated, at the edge of open country. Where the road ends at a turning point, double back left on a forestry track climbing through pines and larches, signposted 'Whinstone Lee Tor'. The track emerges from the shade of the forest out on to Lead Hill, where Ladybower Reservoir and the sombre sprawl of Bleaklow come into view.

WHERE TO EAT AND DRINK

There is nowhere to eat and drink en route. The nearest pub is the Ladybower Inn, a short way east along the A57. The Yorkshire Bridge Inn, about 0.5 mile (800m) south on the A6013 towards Bamford, is a popular and welcoming pub, serving a good range of bar and restaurant meals every lunchtime and evening.

3 The path keeps the intake wall to the left as it rakes up the bracken slopes of Lead Hill. Follow the well-worn path away from the wall up to the ridge. At the six-way junction of tracks at the top go second left to reach Whinstone Lee Tor.

4 The path continues along the peaty ridge past the Hurkling Stones to an unnamed summit. Beyond this it meets a signposted path heading from Ladybower over to Moscar. Descend left until you reach a gate at the edge of the open country.

5 Through the gate the path descends westwards and alongside the top wall of a conifer plantation. It fords Grindle Clough's stream beyond another gate and turns left past several stone-built barns. The path, now paved, descends further to join the track running along the east shores of Ladybower Reservoir.

WHAT TO LOOK OUT FOR

The mountain hare is quite common on the moor tops. This is a striking reminder of the upland nature of this landscape. In winter its coat changes to a dirty white, to blend with the snow. When there is no snow, it appears faintly ridiculous. You may also be lucky enough to spot a fox, if it doesn't see you first.

6 It is worth doing a detour here to see the remains of Derwent village, which lies 400yds (366m) north-west along the track at the foot of the Mill Brook clough. When you've seen the old village, retrace your steps along the well-graded track, heading southwards along the shores of the reservoir. After rounding Grainfoot Clough the track passes through woodland to return to Ashopton Viaduct.

WHILE YOU'RE THERE

Visit the spectacular Derwent and Howden reservoir dams. You can drive to Fairholmes car park (where there is a refreshment kiosk), just south of the Derwent dam. The dams, built between 1912 and 1916, were used in training forays by the dambusters of 617 Squadron in preparation for their attack on the Moehne and Eder dams in 1943.

Right: Ladybower Reservoir, Peak District National Park (Walk 3).

WALK 4

Back Tor

If you've got more time to spare why not stay higher for longer, and take in some more of those rocky outcrops.

See map and information panel for Walk 3

DISTANCE *8.75 miles (14km)* **MINIMUM TIME** *4hrs 30min*
ASCENT/GRADIENT *1,270ft (386m)* ▲▲▲ **LEVEL OF DIFFICULTY** +++
PATHS *Peaty moorland paths, some paved, and a reservoir road*
LANDSCAPE *High peaty moorland*

WALK 4 DIRECTIONS (Walk 3 option)

Follow Walk 3 to Point 4, just beyond the Hurkling Stones. Instead of turning left on the Moscar–Ladybower path, stay with the ridge path to the impressive Wheel Stones (Point A), also known as the Coach and Horses.

The path climbs over White Tor and another group of rocks overlooking the hollow of Mill Brook. It then passes the Salt Cellar, which stands among deep heather and rocks to the west of the path.

The paved path continues to Dovestone Tor, where a line of squat cliffs overlooks the reservoirs of the Derwent Valley. Beyond them, alongside the path, are a group of rounded outcrops known as the Cakes of Bread. By now you will have probably stretched your imagination to the limits with names for the numerous rocky outcrops.

The short climb to Back Tor (Point B) ends with a little scramble to get to the trig point, which tops a huge weather-smoothed boulder. The views of Bleaklow and Kinder are the best of the day. After scrambling off the summit, take the flagged path descending north-west to Lost Lad (Point C), where there is a bronze topograph plate marking the summit, and a a sad story of a young shepherd boy who perished here during a blizzard.

Descend westwards from the summit on the bold path down steep grassy slopes. The gradient eases, and the path becomes a rutted grassy track forking left across Green Sitches.

Leave this track at grid ref 182911 for a path forking right to a clearly visible gate and stile. The waymarked path continues heading north-west down a grassy spur before swinging left by a dilapidated wall. Here it descends to a junction of footpaths near the ruins of Bamford House. Go straight over for the steep, winding path down to reach Derwent Reservoir.

Follow the shoreline track southwards, to rejoin Walk 3 at Point 6, by Mill Brook.

Right: Derwent Valley, Peak District National Park (Walk 4)

WALK 5

Ancient Highways to Hope

A linear walk from Edale village to Hope, following in the footsteps of jaggers and Roman Legionnaires.

DISTANCE *7 miles (11.3km)* **MINIMUM TIME** *4hrs*

ASCENT/GRADIENT *656ft (200m)* ▲▲▲ **LEVEL OF DIFFICULTY** +++

PATHS *Well graded, waymarked paths and tracks, several stiles*

LANDSCAPE *High ridge and hillside pastures*

SUGGESTED MAP *OS Explorer OL1 Dark Peak*

START/FINISH *Grid reference: SK 124853*

DOG FRIENDLINESS *Mostly farmland and access agreement land; dogs on lead*

PARKING *Edale village pay car park*

PUBLIC TOILETS *At car park and at Hope village*

WALK 5 DIRECTIONS

Most walkers in Edale will have their eyes to the sky, and their sights on Kinder Scout or Mam Tor. This route's a little different, choosing instead to follow in the footsteps of Roman Legionnaires and jaggers (packhorse drivers of the 16 to 19th century). The jaggers' route stays low on the sides of Kinder Scout before climbing to its high point at Hope Cross where the Roman road to Hope begins.

Turn right out of the car park, heading northwards through the village, under the railway bridge and past The Rambler pub.

Spend a few minutes visiting the National Park's new Moorland Centre (free) then, just beyond it, turn right to follow a sunken walled track through the shade of some trees. This ancient track crosses Grinds Brook before heading eastwards across the fields to the tiny farming hamlet of Ollerbrook Booth. After passing through the farmyard, follow a stony lane that passes Nether Ollerbrook. Take the path passing to the south of Cotefield Farm, through two gates and a stile.

After 200yds (183m), just past a gate and a sign, 'Footpath to Open Country', take the field path on the left, which leaves the track, climbing by a hedge to another footpath signpost. Here the path swings right, above the woods behind Woodhouse Farm.

The path skirts the moor, threading through attractive gorse, bracken and hawthorn trees.

WHILE YOU'RE THERE

While in Hope visit St Peter's Church, which dates back to the 13th century though its spired tower was added in the 14th. The font is Norman, the only thing remaining from the original 13th-century building, while the well-preserved oak pulpit was carved in 1652. There's a fine stained glass window in the rebuilt chancel of 1882. Going back outside to the churchyard you'll see the shaft of a Saxon cross.

WHAT TO LOOK OUT FOR

Hope Cross, marked as a stone guidepost on the map, lies 300yds (274m) south along the ridge. It is medieval: the 1737 etched in the stone refers to the engraving date of the surrounding parishes' initials. An ancient chapel once stood near by, where a traveller could shelter and be fed.

Suddenly it becomes a smooth grassy path that leads into the car park of Edale Youth Hostel at Rowland Cote. Pass immediately in front of the youth hostel and, at the far side, descend some steps to cross a footbridge over Lady Brook Clough.

The path now climbs away from the stream and contours round bracken-cloaked hill slopes back into the main valley where it climbs the grassy lower slopes by a dry-stone wall then descends to reach another stream above Clough Farm.

Continuing on its course between field and moor the path, now a wide engineered track, descends into Jaggers Clough, where the recently planted trees of Backside Wood make a pleasant change from most modern conifer plantations. The track climbs out of the clough to the rough pastured ridge that separates Edale from the Woodlands Valley and its finger of Ladybower Reservoir.

On the top there's a five-way junction of tracks. Turn right here, along the Roman road that once linked the forts of Melandra at Glossop and Navio near Bradwell in the Hope valley. From here you're looking down the full length of Edale, whose fields chequered with hawthorn, are enclosed by the rugged, crag-fringed slopes of Kinder Scout and the great grassy hills of the Mam Tor ridge.

After passing Hope Cross, the Roman road forks right, gradually easing away right from the ridge. It soon becomes a stony track, descending the slopes of heather, sedge and bracken. Ahead, you may see the plumes of smoke coming from the chimneys of the Hope cement works.

Past the Brinks, a high cottage on the left, the track has been surfaced with tarmac and lined with trees. It continues the descent to Fulwood Stile Farm.

Leave the lane and follow the signs to walk around the right of the farm buildings. Go through a gate on the right and continue south on a field-edge path. This comes to another lane by the Homestead (a house). Follow the lane beneath the railway, then across the River Noe at Kilhill Bridge. Beyond the bridge the lane climbs out to the main Edale road. Turn left for the last mile (1.6km) into Hope.

On reaching the main road, turn left and then take the second turning on the left for the railway station, where you can catch a train back to Edale.

WHERE TO EAT AND DRINK

Relax at the end of the day at The Rambler at Edale. The big gabled stone pub has a large beer garden and serves delicious bar meals and coffees. Alternatively, if you've time before catching the train back from Hope, try the Woodbine Café, which has always been popular with walkers and does hot pies, bacon sandwiches, cakes and big mugs of tea.

WALK 6

On the Moorland's Edge

To Lantern Pike and Middle Moor above Hayfield in the Sett Valley.

DISTANCE *7 miles (11.3km)* **MINIMUM TIME** *4hrs*

ASCENT/GRADIENT *1,640ft (500m)* ▲▲▲ **LEVEL OF DIFFICULTY** +++

PATHS *Good paths and tracks, plenty of stiles*

LANDSCAPE *Heather moorland, and rolling farm pastures*

SUGGESTED MAP *OS Explorer OL1 Dark Peak*

START/FINISH *Grid reference: SK 036869*

DOG FRIENDLINESS *Walk is on farmland and access agreement land, dogs should be kept on lead*

PARKING *Sett Valley Trail pay car park, Hayfield*

PUBLIC TOILETS *At car park*

Hayfield was busy. It had cotton mills, papermaking mills and calico printing and dye factories. Hayfield had times of trouble. Floods washed away three bridges, even swept away some bodies from their churchyard graves. And in 1830 it resounded to the marching feet of a thousand protesting mill workers, demanding a living wage. As was always the case in such times, the men were beaten back by soldiers and charged with civil disorder. Their industry went into a slow decline that would last a century, and Hayfield returned to its countryside ways.

The Sett Valley Trail

The first part of the walk to little Lantern Pike follows the Sett Valley Trail, the trackbed of a railway that until 1970 linked Manchester and New Mills with Hayfield. At its peak the steam train would have brought thousands of people from Manchester. Today it's a pleasant tree-lined track, working its way through the valley between the hills of Lantern Pike and Chinley Churn. The track, and its former wasteland surroundings, are becoming quite a haven for wildlife. Beneath the ash, sycamore, beech and oak you'll see wood anemone, bluebells and wild garlic along with the rhubarb-like butterbur. In the days before fridges butterbur leaves were used to wrap butter to keep it cool.

Lantern Pike

Lantern Pike is the middle of three ridges peeping through the trees, and by the time you get to Birch Vale you're ready to tackle it. You ascend on a shady path through woods, then a country lane with wild flowers in the verges, and finally on heather and grass slopes to the rocky-crested summit. Lantern Pike's name comes from the beacon tower that once stood on its summit. It had to be demolished in 1907 after falling into a dangerous state of disrepair. Having descended back down to the busy Glossop road the route then climbs up across Middle Moor where it enters a new landscape – one of expansive heather fields. Soon you're on the skyline looking down on the Kinder and the ever-so-green valley beneath your feet. This seems to be complemented to perfection by the shapely and ever-so-green peaks of Mount Famine and South Head.

Into Modern Hayfield

You come down to Hayfield on the Snake Path, an old traders' route linking the Sett and Woodland valleys. A fine street of stone-built cottages, with window boxes overflowing with flowers, takes you to the centre. This is a place where walkers come, and motorists take tea before motoring somewhere else. It's all so very peaceful – now.

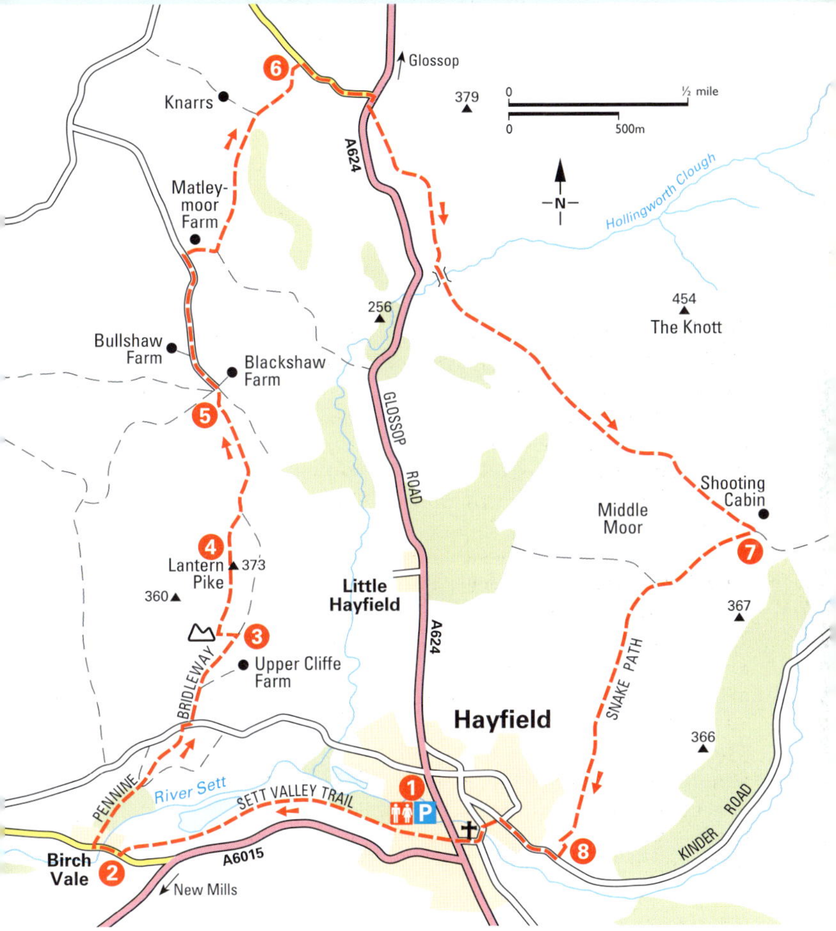

WALK 6 DIRECTIONS

1 Follow the old railway trackbed signed 'The Sett Valley Trail and Pennine Bridleway', from the car park in Hayfield. This heads west down the valley and above the River Sett to meet a minor road close to the A6015 New Mills road at Birch Vale.

2 Turn right along the road, then right again along a cobbled track behind the cottages of the Crescent into the shade of woods. Beyond a gate, the track meets a tarred farm lane at a hairpin bend. Follow the higher course to reach a country lane. Staggered to the right across it, a surfaced lane climbs further up the hillside. Take the left fork near Upper Cliffe Farm to a gate at the edge of the National Trust's Lantern Pike site.

3 Leave the bridleway here and turn left along a grassy wallside path climbing heather and bracken slopes to the rock-fringed ridge. Turn right and climb the airy crest to Lantern Pike's summit, which is topped by a view indicator.

WHERE TO EAT AND DRINK

The Royal Hotel in Hayfield is spacious, comfortable and welcomes hungry walkers and families. Food is served daily in the bar and restaurant, and there's patio seating outside.

4 From here, the path continues northwards from the top of Lantern Pike, descending to a gate at the northern boundary of the National Trust estate, where it rejoins the track you left earlier. Follow this northwards across high pastures to a five-way footpath signpost to the west of Blackshaw Farm.

5 Turn left along the walled farm lane past Bullshaw Farm, then right on a track passing the buildings of Matleymoor Farm. Where the track swings to the right leave it for a rough grassy track on the left. Go over the stile at its end and continue northwards on a grooved path, which joins a semi-surfaced track from Knarrs.

6 At the end turn right and walk along the road to reach the A624 road. Cross this with care and go over the stile at the far side. Turn

WHAT TO LOOK OUT FOR

Lantern Pike was donated to the National Trust in 1950, after being purchased by subscription. It was to be a memorial to Edwin Royce, who fought for the freedom to roam these hills. A summit view indicator, commemorating her life, records the 360-degree panorama.

immediately right, following a faint, rutted track with a wall on the right-hand side. This crosses the little valley of Hollingworth Clough on a footbridge before climbing up the heather slopes of Middle Moor.

7 Near a white shooting cabin, turn right on the stony Snake Path, which descends through heather at first, then, beyond a kissing gate, across fields to reach a stony walled track. Follow it down to Kinder Road near the centre of Hayfield.

WHILE YOU'RE THERE

Take a look round Hayfield. It has many old houses, former industrial mills and cottages. The Pack Horse Inn on Kinder Road dates back to 1577. The Royal Hotel was visited by John Wesley in 1755 when it was still the local parsonage.

8 Turn right down the lane, then left down steps to Church Street. Turn left to St Matthew's Church, then right down a side street signed to the Sett Valley Trail. This leads to the busy main road. Cross with care back to the car park.

In the Footsteps of the Trespass

A dramatic route to Kinder Downfall follows the famous trespassers of 1932.

DISTANCE *8 miles (12.9km)* **MINIMUM TIME** *5hrs*

ASCENT/GRADIENT *1,450ft (440m)* ▲▲▲ **LEVEL OF DIFFICULTY** +++

PATHS *Well-defined tracks and paths, quite a few stiles*

LANDSCAPE *Heather and peat moorland and farm pastures*

SUGGESTED MAP *OS Explorer OL1 Dark Peak*

START/FINISH *Grid reference: SK 048869*

DOG FRIENDLINESS *Walk is on farmland and access agreement land, dogs should be kept on lead*

PARKING *Bowden Bridge pay car park*

PUBLIC TOILETS *Across bridge from car park*

If you want to climb one of the quieter ways to Kinder Scout, Hayfield to the west is one of the best places to start. It's also a route with a bit of history to it. From the beginning of the 20th century there had been conflict between ramblers and the owners of Kinder's moorland plateau. By 1932 ramblers from the industrial conurbations of Sheffield and Manchester, disgusted by lack of government action to open up the moors to walkers, decided to hold a mass trespass on Kinder Scout. Benny Rothman, a Manchester rambler and a staunch communist, would lead the trespass on Sunday 24 April. The police expected to intercept Benny at Hayfield railway station, but he outwitted them by arriving on his bicycle, not in the village itself, but at Bowden Bridge Quarry to the east. Here he was greeted by hundreds of cheering fellow ramblers. With the police in hot pursuit the group made their way towards Kinder Scout.

Although they were threatened and barracked by a large gathering of armed gamekeepers the ramblers still managed to get far enough to join their fellow trespassers from Sheffield, who had come up from the Snake Inn. Predictably, fighting broke out and Benny Rothman was one of five arrested. He was given a four-month jail sentence for unlawful assembly and breach of the peace. The ramblers' cause inspired folk singer, Ewan McColl (famous for *Dirty Old Town* and *The First Time Ever I Saw Your Face*) to write *The Manchester Rambler*, which became something of an anthem for the proliferating walkers' clubs and societies. However it took until 1951, when the recently formed National Park negotiated access agreements with the landowners, for the situation to improve.

Just like the mass trespass this walk starts at Bowden Bridge, where you will see a commemorative plaque on the rock face above the car park. After climbing through the Kinder Valley and above Kinder Reservoir you're confronted by those same moors of purple heather and the enticing craggy sides of the Scout. But now it is the National Park signs that greet you, not a gun-toting gamekeeper.

The Downfall

A dark shadow-filled cleft in the rocks is the Kinder Downfall, where the infant Kinder tumbles off the plateau. Now you climb to the edge for the most spectacular part of the walk – the trespass – and continue along a promenade of dusky gritstone rock. Round the next corner you come to that dark cleft seen earlier. In the dry summer months the fall is a mere trickle, but after the winter rains it can turn into a 100ft (30m) torrent. The prevailing west wind often catches the torrent, funnelling it back up to the top rocks like plumes of white smoke. In contrast, the way down is gentle, leaving the edge at Red Brook and descending the pastures of Tunstead Clough Farm. A leafy lane takes you back into the Kinder Valley.

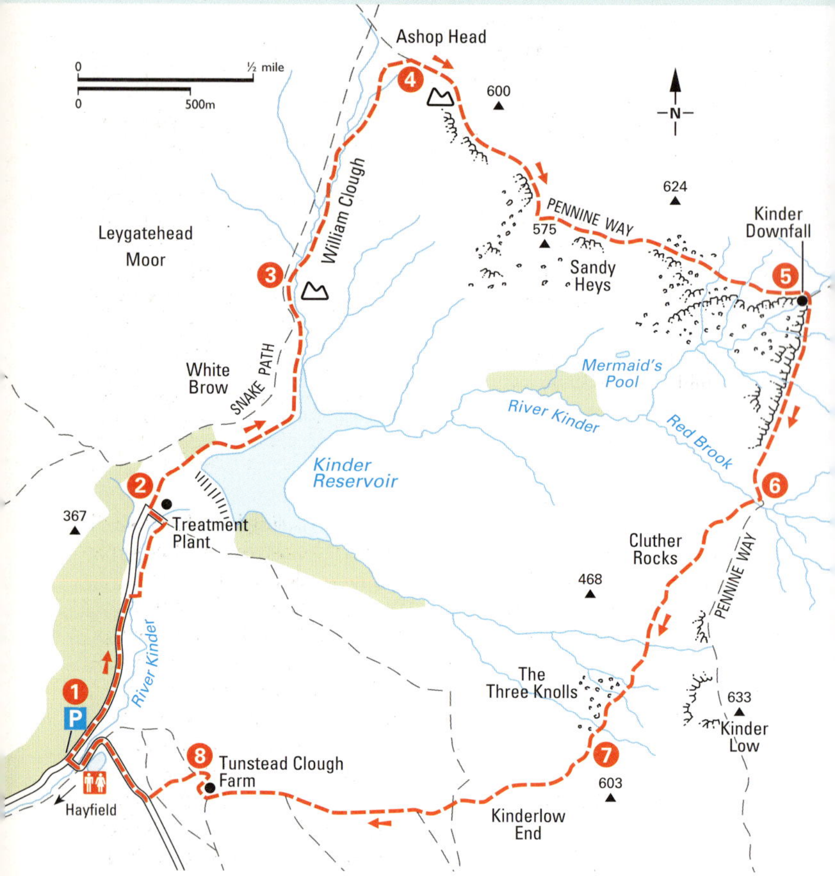

WALK 7 DIRECTIONS

1 Turn left out of the car park and walk up the lane, which winds beneath the trees and by the banks of the River Kinder. After 550yds (503m), leave the lane at a signposted footpath after crossing a bridge. Follow the path as it traces the east bank of the river before turning left to rejoin the road at a point just short of the treatment plant buildings.

2 Here you fork left through a gate on to a cobbled bridleway, climbing above the buildings. It continues alongside the reservoir's

WHERE TO EAT AND DRINK

Near the car park on Kinder Road, The Sportsman is a walker-friendly pub, which serves hot and cold food every lunchtime and evening – from snacks to main meals. Children and dogs are welcome and there's a pleasant outside seating area.

north shore, turning sharp left on White Brow. Beyond a gate, but don't cross over the footbridge, follow the path instead as it climbs alongside William Clough, where it is joined by the Snake Path from the left.

3 The path crosses and recrosses the stream as it works its way up the grass and heather clough. In the upper stages the narrowing clough loses its vegetation and the stream becomes a trickle in the peat. Climb to Ashop Head where you meet the Pennine Way at a crossroads of paths.

4 Turn right to walk along the slabbed Pennine Way path across the moor towards Kinder Scout's north-west edge, then climb those last gritstone slopes on a pitched path to gain the summit plateau. Now it's easy walking along the edge.

5 After turning left into the rocky combe of the River Kinder, the Mermaid's Pool and the Kinder Downfall (waterfalls) come into view. Descend to cross the Kinder's shallow rocky channel about 100yds (91m) back from the edge before turning right and continuing along the edge.

WHILE YOU'RE THERE

In 2007, the 75th anniversary of the mass trespass was marked by the opening of the Trespass Trail, a 14-mile (22.6km) walk following the route of the original brave trespassers up on to Kinder Scout. A booklet guide is available from Hayfield Information Centre.

6 Beyond Red Brook, leave the plateau by taking the right fork, which descends south-westwards, contouring round grassy slopes beneath the rocky edge.

WHAT TO LOOK OUT FOR

When you're absorbed in the cerebral pleasures of wilderness walking, some comic bird with a flash of red on his head will probably wreck the moment by cackling loudly before scuttling from under your feet. This red grouse will have been absorbed in the pleasures of the tasty heather shoots you are passing. The gamekeeper makes sure that this ungainly bird has all he needs to breed successfully – a mixture of young heather and mature plants for cover.

7 After passing The Three Knolls rocks and swinging right beneath the slopes of Kinderlow End, go through a gate in a fence (grid reference 066867) before taking a right fork to reach another gate in the wall dividing the moor and farmland. Go over a stile next to it and then turn left through a gateway. Descend the trackless pastured spur, passing through several gates and stiles at the field boundaries to pass to the left of Tunstead Clough Farm.

8 Turn right beyond the farmhouse to follow a winding track that descends into the upper Sett Valley. At the crossroads of lanes at the bottom, go straight ahead, and along the road to emerge at Bowden Bridge.

WALK 8

Pennine Ways on Kinder Scout

One end of the famous long distance trail ascends to the craggy outcrops of the Kinder Plateau.

DISTANCE *7 miles (11.3km)* **MINIMUM TIME** *4hrs*

ASCENT/GRADIENT *1,650ft (500m)* ▲▲▲ **LEVEL OF DIFFICULTY** +++

PATHS *Rock and peat paths, some steep ascents and descents*

LANDSCAPE *Heather moor*

SUGGESTED MAP *OS Explorer OL1 Dark Peak*

START/FINISH *Grid reference: SK 125853*

DOG FRIENDLINESS *Walk is on farmland and access agreement land. Dogs should be kept on leads.*

PARKING *Edale pay car park*

PUBLIC TOILETS *At car park*

Edale sits peacefully in a paradise of pasture, riverside meadow and hedgerow, surrounded by high peaks. It's church spire towers above the cottages and farmhouses of its five scattered booths, but is in turn dwarfed by the castellated crags of Kinder Scout, and the rounded hills of the Mam Tor ridge.

In depression torn 1930s England, Tom Stephenson, then secretary of the Ramblers' Association told the readers of the *Daily Herald* of his dream – to create a long, green trail across the roof of England. This dream would bring Edale to the world's attention. It took 30 years, a mass trespass and Acts of Parliament to achieve, but in 1965, the Pennine Way was opened. Spanning 268 miles (429km) from Edale to Kirk Yetholm in Scotland, it was Britain's first official long distance trail. Go to Edale any Friday night and you'll see eager-eyed Pennine Wayfarers. They'll be in the campsite making their last minute preparations, or in the Old Nags Head poring over Ordnance Survey maps or looking though Alfred Wainwright's famous little blue guidebook.

Popular Trail

Unfortunately the popularity of the Way has led to the main route through Grindsbrook being diverted along the foul weather route up Jacob's Ladder. But as you leave Edale, or to be more strictly correct Grindsbrook Booth (Edale is the name of the valley), you can look across to the old route, which delves deep into the rocky ravine. Your route climbs boldly to the top of Ringing Roger (the echoing rocks). From this great viewpoint you can look down on the length of Edale and across to the great Lose Hill–Mam Tor ridge.

What follows is an edge walk round the great chasm of Grindsbrook, taking you past Nether Tor to the place where the old Pennine Way track comes to meet you. The Way didn't bother with the comforts of the edge, but got stuck into those peat hags to the right. It was a stiff navigational challenge to get to the Kinder Downfall on the other side of the expansive plateau. Past weather-smoothed gritstone sculptures and the rocky peak of Grindslow Knoll you come to another ravine, Crowden Brook. This route descends by the brook, passing several waterfalls and offering many chances for a paddle to cool those hot feet. Beneath the open slopes the path seeks the shade of recently planted pine, larch, birch and oak. Colourful wild flowers, including bluebells, daffodils and primroses, proliferate in this delightful spot, just above Upper Booth. Finally you're reacquainted with the Pennine Way, following the new route back across the fields of Edale.

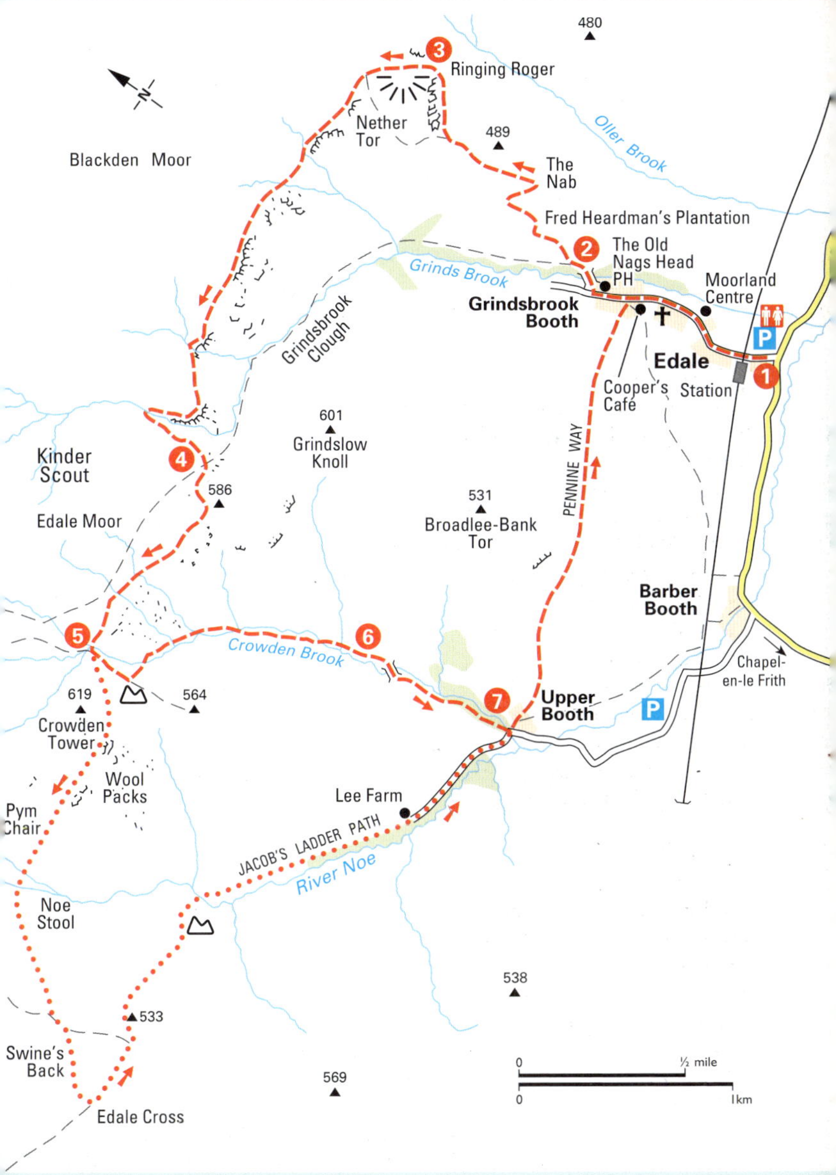

WALK 8

WALK 8 DIRECTIONS

1 Turn right out of the car park and head north into Edale (the village), under the railway and past The Old Nags Head pub. By a gate at the far end turn right and then follow the path across the footbridge that leads over Grinds Brook.

2 Leave the main Grindsbrook Clough path by the side of a small barn, taking the right fork that climbs up the lower hillslope to reach a stile on the edge of open country. Beyond the stile the path zig-zags above Fred Heardman's Plantation then climbs up the nose of The Nab to the skyline rocks. Where the path divides, take the rather eroded right fork to the summit of Ringing Roger.

3 Follow the edge path left, rounding the cavernous hollow of Grindsbrook past Nether Tor. The old Pennine Way route is met on the east side, at a place marked by a large cairn.

4 Ignoring the left fork heading for the outlier of Grindslow Knoll, follow the paved footpath westwards to the head of another deep hollow, the clough of Crowden Brook.

5 Cross Crowden Brook, then leave the edge to follow a narrow level path traversing slopes on the left beneath the imposing outcrop of Crowden Tower. Below the tower, turn left for a steep, bumpy track down the grassy hillside to the brook. Keep to the path that follows the brook, fording it on several occasions.

WHERE TO EAT AND DRINK

The Old Nags Head, or The Rambler at Edale both serve good bar meals, or drinks and snacks are available at Cooper's Cafe by Edale Post Office.

6 Go over a stile at the edge of open country, then cross a footbridge shaded by tall rowans to change to the west bank. From here the path threads through woodland before descending in steps to the road at Upper Booth. You now need to follow the Pennine Way path back to Edale.

7 Turn left along the road and left again into the farmyard of Upper Booth Farm before exiting at the top right corner. After following a track to a gateway, bear left uphill to a stile by an old barn. Here the Way traverses fields at the foot of Broadlee Bank before joining a tree-lined track into the village. Turn right along the road back to the car park.

WHAT TO LOOK OUT FOR

You walk along the edge of Kinder Scout's summit peat bogs. Peat was formed by mosses such as the bright green sphagnum moss you'll see on wet patches. The moss cover is now restricted to small patches. It has been replaced by sedges, grasses, heather and bilberry in a vegetation cover riven by deep and numerous hags in which the naked peat comes to the surface. The base of the hag has often been eroded to the gravelly surface of the core rocks, caused by years of industrial pollution and over-grazing by sheep. However, efforts are being made to restore this fragile habitat. To find out more visit the new Moorland Centre at Edale near the start of the walk.

Jacob's Ladder

Visit more of the plateau's bizarre outcrops in a longer moorland walk.

See map and information panel for Walk 8

DISTANCE *9 miles (14.5km)* **MINIMUM TIME** *5hrs 30min*
ASCENT/GRADIENT *1,650ft (500m)* ▲▲▲ **LEVEL OF DIFFICULTY** +++

WALK 9 DIRECTIONS (Walk 8 option)

This extension to Walk 8 visits more rock architecture on this high moorland plateau. Follow Walk 8 to Crowden Brook (Point 5), but this time stay with the edge path to the top of the Crowden Tower cliffs.

The path now swings right through a fascinating collection of weather-smoothed gritstone outcrops known as the Wool Packs, but sometimes referred to as Whipsnade, because of their likeness to zoo animals.

Continue on the route along the edge past the gigantic Pagoda Rocks and Pym Chair. The latter is a natural rock-seat, dedicated to the 17th-century Parliamentarian, John Pym.

The distinctive angular peak ahead is known as the Swine's Back, such a contrast from the dark peat hags of the Kinder plateau, which rises barely a few feet higher on the right. In winter those few feet take you into an uninviting peat mire. In the drier periods of summer, however, the peat goes flaky. It offers a not unpleasant springy surface for peak-baggers who want to make a detour north-west in search of the pile of stones marking the 636m summit.

The main route now rounds the head of Edale. At Noe Stool, a huge perch overlooking the source of the River Noe, the path follows an old wall on the left beneath the Edale Rocks and Swine's Back. Ignore the inviting short-cut path descending left, but instead follow the wall down to Edale Cross. This rugged gritstone cross marks the highest point on the old packhorse trail between Edale and the Sett Valley. Jacob Marshall one of the traders, lived at nearby Edale Head House (now in ruins). He pioneered the Jacob's Ladder short cut down to the old packhorse bridge, while his heavily laden mules took the longer route to the right.

Turn left to descend the old trail, which has now been adopted by the Pennine Way. A pitched staircase path takes the route downhill to the old bridge where a cart track continues to Lee Farm and a lane to Upper Booth (Point 7). From here follow Walk 8 back to Edale village.

CASTLETON

Over the Shivering Mountain

A ridge walk over the summit of Mam Tor.

DISTANCE *5 miles (8km)* **MINIMUM TIME** *3hrs 30min*
ASCENT/GRADIENT *1,150ft (350m)* ▲▲▲ **LEVEL OF DIFFICULTY** +++
PATHS *Good tracks all the way*
LANDSCAPE *Grassy ridge and farm pastures*
SUGGESTED MAP *OS Explorer OL1 Dark Peak*
START/FINISH *Grid reference: SK 149829*
DOG FRIENDLINESS *Dogs could run free on Hollowford Road*
PARKING *Castleton village pay car park*
PUBLIC TOILETS *At car park*

WALK 10 DIRECTIONS

Mountain walks are seldom as easy to follow as this one to Mam Tor, there are lanes and paved paths for most of the way. From the moment you reach Hollins Cross, you're walking the skyline on easy ridges, with views as good as any in Derbyshire.

Take the tarmac ginnel from the back of the car park, then turn left along Millbridge, which soon becomes Hollowford Road. The route you are about to walk as far as Hollins Cross is a former packhorse route, once used by workers making a daily trip between Castleton and Edale Mill.

The lane climbs the hillside north-west of the village, and passes an outdoor centre. Abandon the lane where it turns sharp left and becomes an unsurfaced track to Woodseats Farm. Go through the gate ahead on to a sunken stony path that leads the route through the shade of hawthorn trees to reach a gate on the edge of the moor. From here you traverse left across the steeper rugged ground of the upper slopes to reach the high pass at Hollins Cross. Here there's a view recorder and monument to rambler Tom Hyett.

You now have the fields of Edale spread beneath your feet. The spire of the village church looks minute when compared with the rock-crested heather slopes of Kinder Scout.

You may hear the whistling of the Manchester train as it hurries through the valley on its way to Sheffield. Follow the paved ridge path left and up to the summit of

WHAT TO LOOK OUT FOR

Take a look at Mam Tor's 'shivering face'. You will be able to see the layers of grits and shales that make the hillside so unstable. When you look over the edge (don't get too close), you'll see the huge landslips below, including the crumbling remains of the old A625 road that went down with them.

WHERE TO EAT AND DRINK

The Castle in Castle Street, Castleton is open all day and serves a range of snacks and main meals. This 17th-century inn is also reputed to be haunted by several ghosts!

Mam Tor. Mam Tor is ringed by a fort dating back to the Bronze Age. The burial mound on the summit was getting so eroded that the National Trust has completely covered it with cobblestones.

The summit is made up of layered shale and gritstone, an unstable surface that has been weathered into flaky cliffs, which give Mam Tor its alternative name, the 'Shivering Mountain'.

From the summit continue along the paved path to the road at Mam Nick, then turn left for the gated path straight down the grassy hillside. Cross the road for the track opposite, fork left via Windy Knoll Cave and down to cross the road once more for a field path past Winnats Head Farm. Beyond the farm descend the narrow lane into the spectacular limestone ravine of Winnats Pass – a 1-in-5 (20%) gradient.

Once a jaggers' track ('jaggers' were the old packhorse train drivers), the Winnats road became an important turnpike in 1758, but this state was short-lived. The Manchester and Sheffield Turnpike Company replaced the tortuous Winnats with the ill-fated Mam Tor road. Unfortunately the Shivering Mountain shivered a little too much for this new road. There were five separate landslips, and repairs were often necessary. Finally in 1977 the road was closed to traffic for good.

It is not necessary to walk on the tarmac through Winnats – there's a good path which descends the grassy slopes beneath the crags on the left all the way down to Speedwell Cavern.

On the far side of the main Speedwell Cavern building, a footpath on the right leads through the National Trust's Longcliff Estate. It skirts the slopes, and roughly follows the line of a dry-stone wall on the left to terminate at Goosehill Farm.

Here continue along the lane, Goosehill, which heads back towards the centre of Castleton. After crossing Goosehill Bridge over Mill Stream, turn left down a tarmac path that follows the stream banks, emerging at the main street opposite the car park.

WHILE YOU'RE THERE

Have a closer look at the Odin Mine, one of the oldest lead mines in Derbyshire. It takes its name from Woden, the Norse god of War. From the roadside you can see a deep rocky gorge, which at first glance appears to be natural. Closer inspection reveals it to have been gouged out by the miners. The mine extends hundreds of feet under Mam Tor and for centuries gave high yields of lead and also some silver.

WALK 11

Chinley Churn and South Head

Two green hills rise above the Pennine village of Chinley on the edge of the Kinder moors.

DISTANCE *5 miles (8km)* **MINIMUM TIME** *3hrs*

ASCENT/GRADIENT *950ft (290m)* ▲▲▲ **LEVEL OF DIFFICULTY** +++

PATHS *Field paths, quarry and farm tracks, a few stiles*

LANDSCAPE *Hill pastures and moorland*

SUGGESTED MAP *OS Explorer OL1 Dark Peak*

START/FINISH *Grid reference: SK 041827*

DOG FRIENDLINESS *Dogs should be kept on lead*

PARKING *Village car park on Station Road*

PUBLIC TOILETS *None on route*

Stand on the Hayfield to Chapel-en-le-Frith road at Chinley Head and you'll see two fine hills, South Head and Chinley Churn. Both are as green as the little combe of Otter Brook that separates them, and the field boundary walls that are emblazoned on their slopes like spider's webs only accentuate their graceful contours.

Victorian Monuments

The best base for exploring both of these hills is Chinley. Two sweeping curved viaducts that span the valley high above the town's rooftops are a reminder that this was once an important railway town: a junction for Sheffield, Manchester and Derby trains. The Reverend Henry Thorald called the viaducts one of the greatest monuments to Victorian industrial England. At one time over 150 trains a day would have raced through the valley. At its height Chinley Station had a café, a bookstall and bustling waiting rooms on every platform.

On leaving Chinley you are confronted by the rust-coloured crags, known as Cracken Edge. They form the upper of two distinct tiers. When you get closer the crags turn out to be the remains of old gritstone quarries. Further exploration reveals the entrances of shafts dug to extract the best stone; also part of the winding engine that conveyed the stone down to the valley below. Today the scene is one of degeneration, of rusty gears and grassy spoil heaps.

A Magnificent Panorama

When you reach the brow of the hill you're rewarded with a panorama of the second part of the walk. In it Kinder Scout peeps over the grassy peaks of Mount Famine and South Head. A pleasant grass track takes the route down from the edge back to the fields of Otter Brook's upper combe. At Chinley Head you come to a stark stone-built house with a strange name. Facing eastwards, the house catches the first of the morning sunshine that glints over the hilltops. That's why it's called Peep-O-Day. Note the small circular window built to catch those early rays of sunshine.

East of the Combe

The second part of the walk is spent on the eastern side of the combe of the Otter Brook. Another substantial old quarry track takes the route across the lower slopes of Mount Famine to a windswept little pass beneath South Head. From here the Sett Valley and the attractive field patterns surrounding South End farm are hidden by the gritstone rim of Mount Famine and the woods of Kinder Bank. The highland plateau of Kinder Scout has disappeared behind the spur of Kinderlow End. But it's only a matter of a short climb to the summit of South Head at 1,620ft (494m) to bring it all back in to view, and much more, before ending the day with an easy descent back into the valley below using farm tracks and field paths.

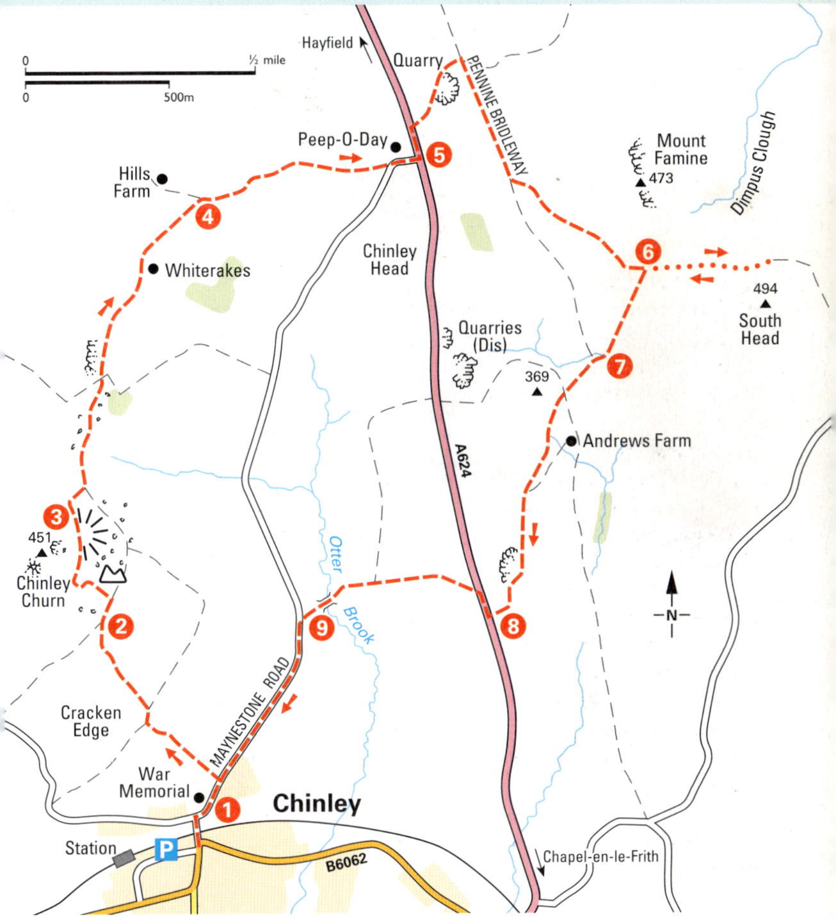

WALK 11 DIRECTIONS

1 From the car park, turn left on Green Lane, then right up Maynestone Road to pass the war memorial. Leave the road for a signed path (grid ref 042828) through a narrow ginnel on the left. Cross a stile, then climb north-west across fields towards Cracken Edge. At a cart track turn right, then left on a path passing between two hillside farmhouses. Go through a gate past the farm on the right before climbing to the lower edge of the quarries.

❷ Swing right on a sketchy path, passing a large hawthorn tree at the base of the grassy hillslope. You join a quarry track that zig-zags up the slope before heading northwards beneath quarry cliffs. Go over the stile in the fence across the track, then climb by this fence to the cliff top.

❸ Turn right along a narrow edge path, then drop down to a wall-walked lower path past the quarried pits. Follow this over a stile and continue beneath the brow of the hill and past Whiterakes cottage.

❹ Turn right on the track from Hills Farm and descend to a tarred lane which passes the evocatively named Peep-O-Day to the A624.

❺ Cross over and turn left along the verge of the busy road. After 150yds (137m) an old cart track on the right goes past a small quarry. Turn right at a T-junction of tracks to follow the Pennine Bridleway across the lower, grassy slopes of Mount Famine.

❻ It's worth making a detour to visit the top of South Head. Simply go through the gate by the National Trust sign and continue on the track to the summit. Resuming the main route, go right over a stile before the gate and descend south-westwards to a walled track.

❼ Follow this down to a crossroads of routes north of Andrews Farm. Go straight on into a field. The path soon develops into a track and joins the descending cart track from Andrews Farm.

❽ On reaching the A624 turn right for 50yds (46m) and then cross to the signposted footpath, which cuts diagonally to the right corner of the first field before following a wall towards Otter Brook. As an old field boundary comes in from the right, the path turns half left to cross over the brook on a slabbed bridge.

❾ A muddy path now climbs half left through scrubby woodland to reach Maynestone Road. Turn left and then follow the road back to Chinley war memorial.

WHERE TO EAT AND DRINK

The Navigation Inn at Whaley Bridge is a cosy little pub with seafaring memorabilia and historical photos on the walls. Its menu consists mainly of traditional, home-cooked meals.

WHILE YOU'RE THERE

Have a look around Buxworth, a village a mile (1.6km) or so west of Chinley. This was once a busy inland port and a terminus for the Peak Forest Tramway and the Peak Forest Canal. These pre-railway industrial transport routes were built in 1806 to link the Peak District with the River Mersey.

Alport's Castles in the Clouds

From historic Fairholmes in the Derwent Valley up to the towering rocky pinnacles of Alport Castles.

DISTANCE *8 miles (12.9km)* **MINIMUM TIME** *5hrs 30min*

ASCENT/GRADIENT *2,000ft (610m)* ▲▲▲ **LEVEL OF DIFFICULTY** +++

PATHS *Well-defined paths and tracks in forests and on moorland*

LANDSCAPE *Afforested hillsides and peaty moorland*

SUGGESTED MAP *OS Explorer OL1 Dark Peak*

START/FINISH *Grid reference: SK 173893*

DOG FRIENDLINESS *Much of the walk is across farmland and access agreement land, dogs should be kept on lead*

PARKING *Fairholmes pay car park*

PUBLIC TOILETS *At car park*

The walk begins in the Derwent Valley, beneath the great stone ramparts of the impressive Derwent Dam. Fairholmes car park has a history all of its own. At the south end the crumbling foundations of Fairholmes Farm are an evocative reminder that this was once agricultural land. During the construction of the reservoirs the upper car park was a masons' yard reverberating to the sounds of workmen cutting, shaping and dressing stone for the dams. The stone came from the Longshaw quarry and was transported here by a specially constructed railway, which linked with the LMS sidings in Bamford.

England's Largest Landslip

You don't stay long in the valley – the route has higher things in mind, and climbs through Lockerbrook Coppice. After emerging from the trees, the route follows the top edge of the vast Hagg Side spruce plantation before climbing to Bellhag Tor. Here you get the first view of the landslips that have occurred in the region. However, by climbing north-west along the peaty ridge of Rowlee Pasture, England's largest landslip will be revealed beneath your feet. They call it Alport Castles and, as you stand on the edge of the cliff looking across to the Tower, you can see why. A huge gritstone tor towers above a chaotic jumble of tumbled boulders and the grassy mounds that have been separated from the main ridge. The reason for the instability lies in the shales that are squeezed between the tiers of gritstone here. In wetter times, after the last ice age, the river eroded these soft bands, resulting in a 0.5 mile (800m) long landslide that dropped 100ft (30m) below the main cliff.

Secret Lovefeast

Looking across the Castle your eye is led to the great straw-coloured expanses of Bleaklow, but we'll save that for another day. Your route takes you on a little path beneath the gritstone walls and down towards Alport Castles Farm in the valley below. On the first Sunday of every July they hold the Woodlands Lovefeast service in the barn. These non-conformist religious ceremonies started during the reign of Charles II. Presbyterianism in such times was against the law, and the services had to be held in remote places, far from the eyes of the King's loyal subjects.

Past the farm you follow the valley to its meeting with the Ashop Valley. Here an old Roman road that linked forts at Melandra, at Glossop, and Navio, near Bradwell, takes you across the lower grassy slopes of Kinder Scout, where a jaggers' track is waiting to take you down to a secluded little packhorse bridge at Haggwater before transporting you over the hill towards Fairholmes.

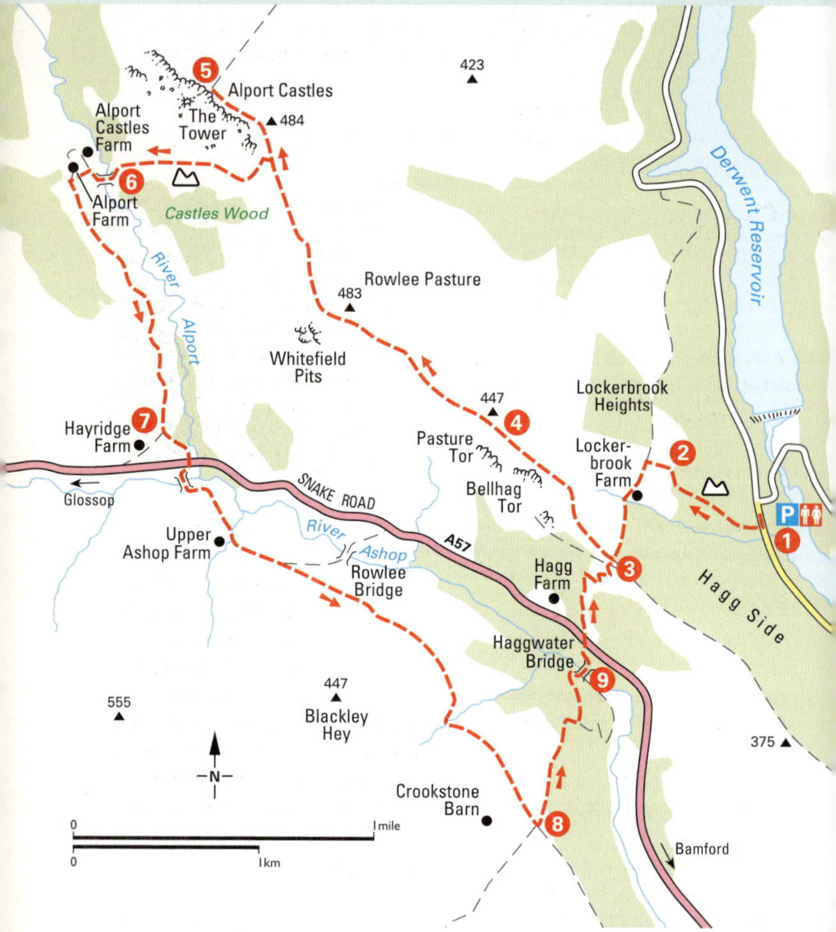

WALK 12 DIRECTIONS

1 Leave the car park for the road, then follow a forestry track, signposted 'Lockerbrook and Derwent Discovery Walk'. It climbs through Hagg Side Wood, crossing the bridge over a water leat before steepening on the higher slopes. Near the top the waymarked path leaves the forest in sight of the farm.

2 An obvious footpath, guided by a stone wall, traverses the fields of Lockerbrook Heights. Turn left

WHILE YOU'RE THERE

Hire a mountain bike from the hire centre in Fairholmes car park. This is an excellent area for cycling and one of the most popular routes is the circuit of the now flooded Derwent Valley. At the head of the valley, at Slippery Stones, is the old packhorse bridge which was once in the village centre. It was dismantled and rebuilt here when the reservoirs were built.

at a public footpath signpost and follow a track southwards past Lockerbrook Farm.

3 On reaching the ridgetop by Woodcock Coppice, turn right along a permissive path climbing to the open moor at Bellhag Tor.

4 Continue over Rowlee Pasture and along a ridgetop path climbing to Alport Castles.

5 Descend on the good path at the southern end of the Castles. Initially the path follows an old wall. On the lower slopes it traces the perimeter of Castles Wood.

6 Cross the footbridge over the River Alport, where the path turns right. Follow the waymarks across a small field. At Alport Farm turn left on the farm drive and then head southwards down the valley.

7 Where the track veers right for Hayridge Farm, leave it for a signed path descending south-east towards the edge of a small riverside wood, to exit on the busy A57 Snake Road. Across the road follow a stony track to the River Ashop, then cross the footbridge to the right of a ford. Rejoin the track, which skirts the hill slopes beneath Upper Ashop Farm before climbing steadily across the rough grassy slopes of Blackley Hey. Ignore the left fork (surfaced drive) descending to Rowlee Bridge, but continue with the track you're on as far as the path intersection to the east of Crookstone Barn.

8 Turn left here on the rutted track along the top edge of the pinewoods before entering them. Leave the track just beyond a right-hand bend and follow a narrow path to Haggwater Bridge.

WHAT TO LOOK OUT FOR

The leat you can see in the woods at Lockerbrook Coppice is part of a complex system of drains and aqueducts which were built to carry excess water from the Ashop and Alport rivers into the neighbouring Derwent reservoirs. This was a skillfully designed network of flowing water and involved the drilling of a tunnel through the side of the mountain from the Woodlands Valley.

9 Beyond the bridge, the path climbs back up again to the A57 Snake Road. Cross the road and join the track opposite. It climbs out of the Woodlands Valley to the east of Hagg Farm and zig-zags across the upper slopes at the edge of Woodcock Coppice before skirting the Hagg Side conifer plantations. Here, retrace your route down through Lockerbrook Coppice to reach the car park.

WHERE TO EAT AND DRINK

You can get hot pies, drinks and snacks at the Fairholmes car park kiosk in spring and summer. The nearest pub is the popular Snake Pass Inn a few miles up the Woodlands Valley at the foot of the notorious A57 Snake Road over the Pennines to Glossop.

The Goyt Valley of the Grimshawes

A Manchester family's country retreat gave way to the inexorable demand for more water.

DISTANCE *3.5 miles (5.7km)* **MINIMUM TIME** *2hrs 30min*

ASCENT/GRADIENT *984ft (300m)* ▲▲▲ **LEVEL OF DIFFICULTY** +++

PATHS *Good paths and tracks, a few stiles*

LANDSCAPE *Park type woodland and moor*

SUGGESTED MAP *OS Explorer OL24 White Peak*

START/FINISH *Grid reference: SK 012748*

DOG FRIENDLINESS *Dogs should be kept under close control*

PARKING *Errwood car park*

PUBLIC TOILETS *1 mile (1.6km) south at Derbyshire Bridge car park*

The River Goyt begins its journey on the wild heather moors of Axe Edge and Goyt Moss before flowing northwards to join the Mersey at Stockport. In times past its remote upper valley would have been filled with oakwoods. An old salters' and smugglers' road known as the Street, straddled it at Goyt Bridge before climbing over the Shining Tor ridge at Pym Chair (a different one to that mentioned in Walk 9).

Errwood Hall

In 1830, the rich Manchester industrialist, Samuel Grimshawe, chose this remote valley to build Errwood Hall, as a wedding present for his son. Taking advantage of its relative isolation, the family lived here 'in the style of princes'. They imported 40,000 rhododendrons and azaleas for the ornate gardens, using their own ocean yacht, *Mariquita*. In its heyday the estate had a staff of 20, and included a coal mine, a water mill, housing for the servants and a private school.

But even the Grimshawes and all their accumulated wealth couldn't resist Stockport's ever-growing need for water, and in 1938 the house was demolished for the newly-built Fernilee Reservoir. The dark battalions of spruce and larch, planted for a quick and plentiful supply of timber, eventually engulfed the oakwoods, and 30 years later a second reservoir, the Errwood, was built, higher up the valley. Little Goyt Bridge was dismantled and rebuilt upstream; and the valley was changed forever. For a while it became the destination of seemingly every Sunday car outing from Greater Manchester. The valley's single road was choked by vehicles and that remoteness and quiet seemed lost forever. Then a pioneering traffic management scheme was initiated by the National Park authority, including new car parks, a bus service and even road closures. The result was that this once peaceful beauty spot was restored to a state of relative tranquillity.

Back to the Grimshawes

This walk takes you back to the 19th century, to the time of the Grimshawes, but first you aim to get an overview of the valley by climbing the grassy spur dividing the Goyt and Shooter's Clough. After dropping into Shooter's Clough the path wanders through unruly streamside woodland to green pastures and a wooded knoll. You briefly rejoin the crowds on the way to Errwood Hall. As you enter the grounds the order of the garden has been ruffled by nature, but the rhododendrons still bloom bright in the summer. The mossy foundations and floors still exist, as do some of the lower walls, arched windows and doors. You leave the hall and the crowds behind to round a wooded hill.

The Spanish Shrine

Uphill in a wild, partially wooded comb lies the Spanish Shrine, built by the Grimshawes in memory of their beloved governess, Dolores de Bergrin. Inside the circular stone-built shrine there is a fine altar and mosaic. If the weather is clement then your spirits will be lifted by the return walk along the crest of Foxlow Edge, for you can see most of today's walk laid beneath your feet as you survey the wild rolling moors, which are dappled with heather, bracken and pale moor grasses. Dinghies may be racing across Errwood Reservoir and even the spruce woods seem to fit into this exquisite jigsaw.

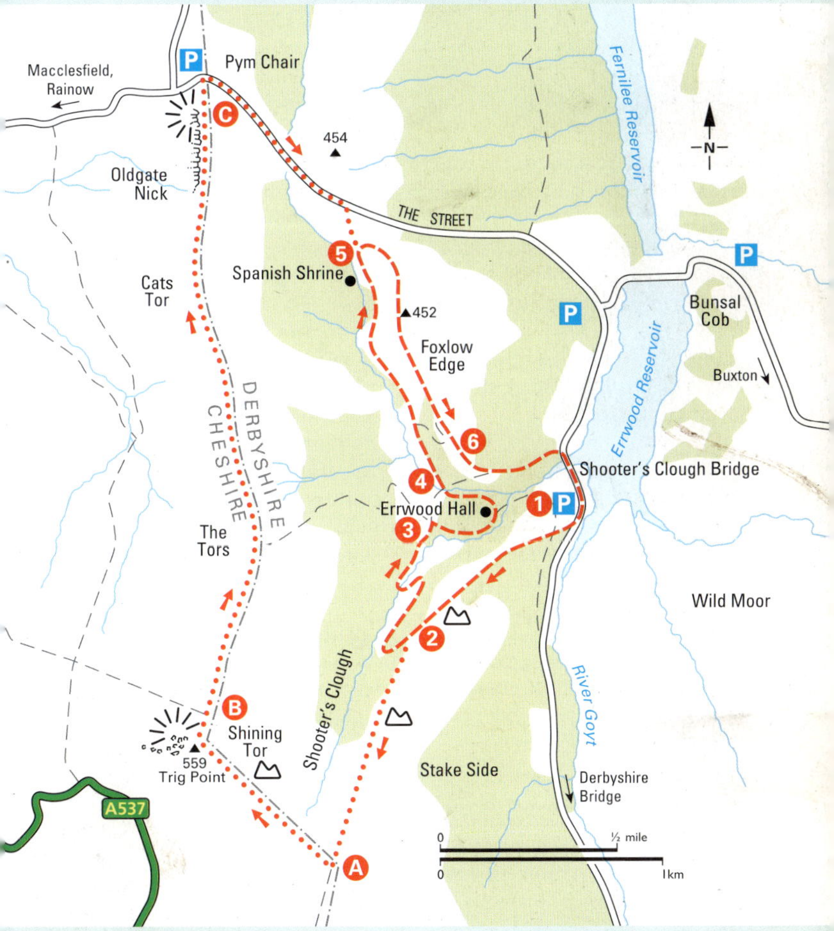

WALK 13 DIRECTIONS

1 The path, signposted to Stakeside and the Cat and Fiddle, begins from the roadside just south of the car park. Climb with this road through a copse of trees, go straight across a cart track, then climb the grassy spur separating Shooter's Clough and the Goyt Valley.

WHERE TO EAT AND DRINK

There's usually an ice cream van in the car park at Errwood in summer, but nothing on the route itself. The Cat and Fiddle Inn is on the Macclesfield–Buxton road, a couple of miles drive away, or try the Shady Oak Inn on the Buxton–Whaley Brige road at Fernilee, which serves food daily.

2 Go through a gate in the wall on the right that runs along the spur and follow a grassy path that zig-zags through the woodland of Shooter's Clough before fording a stream. The path heads north (right), through rhododendron bushes before continuing across open grassland to a signposted junction of footpaths.

3 Turn right here on a good path skirting the near side of a wooded knoll, then ignoring the first path through the gateposts take the

WHAT TO LOOK OUT FOR

On the west slopes of Burbage Edge you'll see the old trackbed of the Cromford and High Peak Railway, from the tunnel near the top down to the shores of Errwood Reservoir. Although this famous railway was one of the earliest in the country, the branch through the Goyt Valley was only in use between 1852 and 1877.

WHILE YOU'RE THERE

Just off the route and to the west of Errwood Hall are the remains of the Grimshawe's burial ground, where you can see the graves of family members, some of their servants and Captain John Butler of their yacht *Mariquita*.

second left to Errwood Hall. The path continues past the ruins, before descending some steps to cross a stream via a footbridge.

4 Climb some steps on the right to reach another footpath signpost. Turn left along the path signposted to Pym Chair. This gradually swings north on hillslopes beneath Foxlow Edge. There's a short detour down and left to see the Spanish Shrine (visible from the main path).

5 About 100yds (91m) on from the Spanish Shrine, and before meeting the road at the very top, the path reaches open moorland. Take the narrow path forking right, which climbs to the top of Foxlow Edge. On reaching some old quarry workings near the top, the path is joined by a tumbledown dry-stone wall. Keep to the narrow corridor between the wall on the right and the fence on your left, ignoring little paths and tracks off to the right down into the valley. Continue the slow descent to the far end of the ridge.

6 At a fence corner, by the edge of woodland follow the path left, still downhill, around the edge of the trees and veer left again where it is joined by another path. With banks of rhododendrons on your right, follow the broad, gravelly track down through the woods to the roadside at Shooter's Clough Bridge. Turn right and cross the road bridge back to the car park.

Shining Tor, Cats Tor and Oldgate Nick

A longer walk taking you into Cheshire with views across to Staffordshire.

See map and information panel for Walk 13

DISTANCE 5.5 miles (9km) **MINIMUM TIME** 3hrs 30min

ASCENT/GRADIENT 1,150ft (350m) ▲▲▲ **LEVEL OF DIFFICULTY** +++

WALK 14 DIRECTIONS (Walk 13 option)

If you want something a bit more challenging from your day in the Goyt Valley, you may feel drawn towards the shapely moorland peaks which rise above the valley's western flank. The views alone make this a worthwhile longer version of Walk 13.

Follow Walk 13 to Point 2 but stay with the wallside path up the spur. At the top, Point A, turn right, through a gate in the wall. You're now walking on the county boundary – moorland on the other side of the wall belongs to Cheshire. Follow the clear gravel path down to a moorland saddle at the head of Shooter's Clough, then up to the top of Shining Tor (Point B). A ladder stile allows you to scale the ridge wall to get to the summit trig point, which lies in Cheshire.

The views are far-reaching and grand. The sprawling heather moorland of Goyt Moss and Axe Edge adds a little colour to the scene in August, but you can't help looking out of Derbyshire to a little pyramid of a peak called Shuttlingsloe, which rises out of the Macclesfield Forest. Still further south, the rocky crests of Hen Cloud and the Roaches make a last defiant stand for the Pennines before dropping into the plains of Staffordshire.

Go back over the ladder stile to the path, which descends northwards to a saddle marked on OS maps as the Torrs. The old path has been eroded into a glutinous peat channel, and all but the purist will be pleased to walk on the gritstone slabs provided by the pathmaker. The path now climbs to Cats Tor where you can look back to Shining Tor, which now shows itself as a sizeable angular escarpment with its own moorland combe.

The path continues over Oldgate Nick to a high moorland road near Pym Chair. This is the old salters' route, known as the Street (Point C). Turn right along the road and descend for about 0.75 mile (1km). Turn right along a signposted footpath. After about 300yds (274m) you'll come to Point 5 on Walk 13. Take the left fork (gently uphill) and follow Walk 13 back to the car park.

WALK 15

Town and Country Manners in Buxton

Through the streets and surrounding countryside of Buxton – spa town and for many the 'Bath of the North'.

DISTANCE *3 miles (4.8km)* **MINIMUM TIME** *2hrs*

ASCENT/GRADIENT *459ft (140m)* ▲▲▲ **LEVEL OF DIFFICULTY** +++

PATHS *Streets and well-defined woodland paths (could be a little muddy in winter), a couple of stiles*

LANDSCAPE *Town and wooded hillside*

SUGGESTED MAP *OS Explorer OL24 White Peak*

START/FINISH *Grid reference: SK 054734*

DOG FRIENDLINESS *Dogs can run free once away from the town streets*

PARKING *Pay car park by the Pavilion*

PUBLIC TOILETS *At car park and at back of Town Hall*

WALK 15 DIRECTIONS

This short walk takes a look at the town from both street level and from a lofty perch in the hills. It explores Buxton's town and surrounding countryside.

From the car park follow the tarmac terrace in front of the Pavilion. This iron and glass building of 1871 includes a hot house with many interesting tropical plants exhibited, and a spa water swimming pool.

The terrace comes out at the square by the fine Edwardian Opera House. Turn right along the square and continue to the Old Hall Hotel. The 6th Earl of Shrewsbury built the original hall in the 16th century and lived here with his wife, Bess of Hardwick. The old hall was incorporated into the present building in 1670. Now turn left past the tourist information centre, which was formerly the Natural Baths building, built in 1851. Next you pass the Crescent, an elegant Georgian terrace designed by John Carr of York and modelled on the Royal Crescent in Bath. On the opposite side of the road is the Pump Room, which served spa water until 1981, and St Anne's Well. The spring that later became St Anne's Well was the one used by Roman legionnaires and later by Mary, Queen of Scots,in an attempt to cure her rheumatism.

Take the tarred path to walk to the left of the pumphouse and follow it up the parkland of the Slopes to the Town Hall. Take the little ginnel that runs to the left of the Town Hall to reach the Market Place. The market cross here dates back to the 15th century,

WHILE YOU'RE THERE

The Buxton Museum and Art Gallery is well worth a visit. Here you can see Roman artefacts from many Derbyshire archaeological digs, and explore the fascinating geology of the Peak. In 1990 it won the Museum of the Year award for its Peak District Display.

WHERE TO EAT AND DRINK

There's a wide choice of pubs and cafés in the town, but at one of the most accessible is the Pavilion Cafe, which serves good food and is open daily all year round.

and originally stood on Cockyard Hill, near where the Palace Hotel stands now. It was moved in 1813 when Buxton was awarded its market charter.

Continue up High Street to Higher Buxton. St Anne's Church on the right is the oldest building in Buxton, dating back to 1625. On reaching a five-way junction, turn half right along Green Lane to its junction with College Road.

Turn left by a public footpath sign for a wide path then go right over a stile on to the recreation ground. Cross over to the far side of the sports pitches.

The continuing path now climbs rough pasture to enter Grin Low Wood. Keep to the southbound path, which climbs to a gate at the top of the plantation. It passes to the right of an old dew pond before making a beeline for Solomon's Temple on the top of the hill. The temple was built in 1896 by Solomon Mycock on the site of a neolithic burial mound, in an exercise to provide work for the unemployed. Now you can see Buxton below you, sheltered beneath the ochre-coloured moors of Combs Moss and Axe Edge.

Descend on the well-used path north-westwards to the woodland's edge. Go through the gate and follow the waymarked path down through the woods to Poole's Cavern car park.

Poole's Cavern, one of the so-called 'Seven Wonders of the Peak', was named after the 'robber Poole', who lived here in the 15th century. Archaeologists have uncovered fascinating relics of Stone and Bronze Age cave dwellers, along with some fine Roman artefacts.

Beyond Poole's Cavern you come to the junction of Temple Road and Green Lane. Go down the former, following it round to the right to a crossroads with the Pavilion Gardens ahead. Follow any one of the many paths across these beautifully laid-out gardens. The pleasant surroundings are a charming reminder of the town's 19th-century heyday. After passing the three lakes and the miniature railway you will reach the Opera House. Turn sharp left here, down the terrace running alongside the Pavilion next door to return to the car park.

WHAT TO LOOK OUT FOR

Take time to look at the buildings. Like many spa towns, Buxton has been very fashionable in the past. Wealthy 'High Society' folk were once enticed to take the hot spa waters and there is a wealth of grand architecture reflecting that prosperity. But the town has also known some very hard times when the spa boom ended and the visitors just stopped coming. Before the restoration programme initiated in the 1980s many of the town's elegant buildings had fallen into decay. Today you can see the tangible benefits of that restoration programme, but there is still an element of faded charm.

Combs Reservoir and Across Dickie's Meadow

A quiet corner of Derbyshire, between the Goyt and Chapel-en-le-Frith.

DISTANCE *3 miles (4.8km)* **MINIMUM TIME** *2hrs 30min*

ASCENT/GRADIENT *164ft (50m)* ▲▲▲ **LEVEL OF DIFFICULTY** +++

PATHS *Can be muddy, quite a few stiles*

LANDSCAPE *Lakes, meadows, and high moors*

SUGGESTED MAP *OS Explorer OL24 White Peak*

START/FINISH *Grid reference: SK 033797*

DOG FRIENDLINESS *Farmland – dogs should be kept on lead*

PARKING *Combs reservoir car park*

PUBLIC TOILETS *None on route*

Combs lies in a quiet corner of north-west Derbyshire, off the road between Chapel-en-le-Frith and Whaley Bridge and beneath the sombre crag-fringed slopes of Combs Moss. This is a fine little corner of Derbyshire, tucked away from the crowds of Castleton and Hathersage.

Combs Reservoir

The route starts by the west side of the dam on a narrow path between the lake and Meveril Brook. Red campion and thickets of dog rose line the path, which rounds the reservoir to its southern tip. You might see a pair of great crested grebes swimming among the rushes. Beyond the reservoir the path tucks under the railway, which brings to mind a mysterious story concerning Ned Dixon, who lived in nearby Tunstead Farm. Ned, or Dickie as he was known, was brutally murdered by his cousin. Locals say his spirit lived on in his skull, which was left outside to guard against intruders. Strange things were said to happen when anybody tried to remove the skull. It is also claimed that the present road from Combs to Chapel was constructed because the railway bridge would not stand over Dane Hey Road. After the first bridge was completed it collapsed, burying the workmen's tools. This was blamed on the skull: Dickie had been against the railway going across Tunstead land.

Combs

A lane with hedges of honeysuckle and hawthorn winds into the village of Combs, where a handful of stone-built cottages are centred on the welcoming Beehive Inn. Combs' most famous son is Herbert Froode. He made his name in automotive engineering as one of the inventors of the brake lining. Starting out in the early 1890s he developed woven cotton brakes for horse-drawn wagons, but his ideas didn't really take off until 1897 when the first motor buses emerged. Froode applied his knowledge of brakes to this much greater challenge and by the end of the century had won a contract to supply brake linings for the new London omnibuses. Ferodo, his company, is an anagram of his surname.

Final Views

Through the village the route takes to the hillsides. Now Combs Reservoir, which is spread beneath your feet, looks every bit a natural lake. Beyond it are the plains of Manchester and the hazy blue West Pennine horizon. In the other direction the gritstone cliffs of Combs Edge, which look rather like those of Kinder Scout, overshadow the sullen combe of Pyegreave Brook.

This very pleasing walk ends as it starts, by the shores of the reservoir. If you look along the line of the dam towards the right of two farms, you'll see where Dickie lived. He's probably watching you, too.

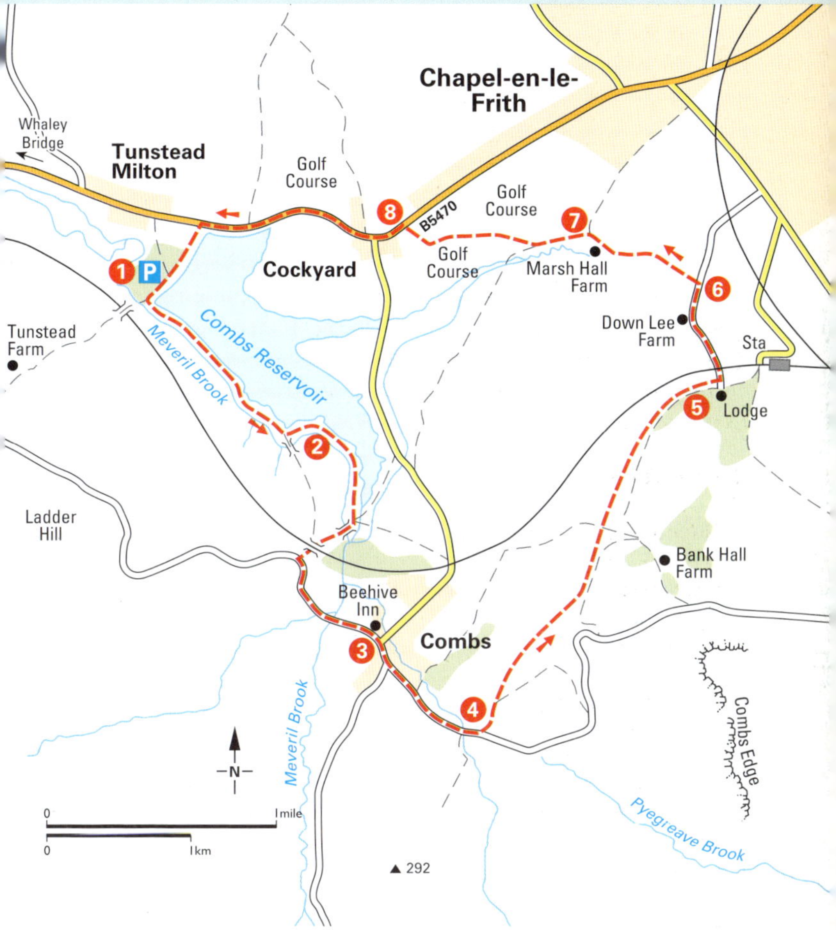

WALK 16 DIRECTIONS

1 Follow the path from the dam along the reservoir's western shore, ignoring the first footbridge over Meveril Brook.

2 As the reservoir narrows the path traverses small fields, then comes to another footbridge over the brook. This time cross it and head south to continue across another field. Beyond a foot tunnel under the Buxton line railway, the path reaches a narrow hedge-lined country lane. Turn left along the lane and continue into Combs village.

3 Past the Beehive Inn in the village centre, take the lane straight ahead, then the left fork, signposted to Dove Holes. This climbs out of the village towards Combs Edge.

WHILE YOU'RE THERE

Take a look around charming Chapel-en-le-Frith, a traditional market town with a cobbled square and the 14th-century Church of St Thomas à Becket. In 1648 1,500 Scottish soldiers were taken prisoner and locked in the church after the Battle of Ribbleton Moor. Forty-eight soldiers died in what was to be known as the Black Hole of Derbyshire.

4 Take the second footpath on the left, which begins at a muddy clearing just beyond Millway Cottage. Go through the stile and climb on a partially slabbed path and then uphill across pasture with the wall on your right. Away to the right is the huge comb of Pyegreave Brook. Climb the pathless spur and go through gateways in the next two boundary walls before following a wall on the right. Ignore a gate in this wall – that's a path to Bank Hall Farm – but stay with the narrow path raking across rough grassy hill slopes with the railway line and the reservoir below left.

5 The path comes down to a track that runs alongside the railway line. This joins a lane just short of the Lodge. Turn left to go under the railway and north to Down Lee Farm.

6 Turn left through a kissing gate 200yds (183m) beyond the farmhouse. The signposted path follows an overgrown hedge towards Marsh Hall Farm. The fields can become very boggy on the final approaches. When you reach the farm complex turn right over a stile and then follow a vehicle track heading in a north-westerly direction.

7 After 200yds (183m) turn left on a field path that heads west to a stile at the edge of the Chapel-en-le-Frith golf course. Waymarking arrows show the way across the fairway. The stile marking the exit from the golf course is 300yds (274m) short of the clubhouse. You then cross a small field to reach the B5470.

8 Turn left to walk along the road (there's a pavement on the far side), and follow it past the Hanging Gate pub at Cockyard. After passing the entrance to the sailing club, turn left to cross over the dam of Combs Reservoir and continue ahead to return to the car park.

WHERE TO EAT AND DRINK

The Beehive Inn at Combs is a splendid little pub serving fine bar meals. Alternatively, there's the more formal Hanging Gate Inn at Cockyard.

WHAT TO LOOK OUT FOR

On a winter's day in 1995 a group of birders saw something they hadn't been expecting. While wandering by the west shores of Combs Reservioir they came across some huge clawed footprints sunk deep into the mud. After studying the photographs they had taken it became obvious that a huge cat had been on the prowl – probably the Peak Panther that has had many sightings locally.

Castles and Caverns

Castleton is where the limestone of the White Peak and the shales and gritstone of the Dark Peak collide.

DISTANCE *5 miles (8km)* **MINIMUM TIME** *3hrs*

ASCENT/GRADIENT *820ft (250m)* ▲▲▲ **LEVEL OF DIFFICULTY** +++

PATHS *Path below Blue John Mines can be tricky in wintry conditions*

LANDSCAPE *Limestone ravines and high pastureland*

SUGGESTED MAP *OS Explorer OL1 Dark Peak*

START/FINISH *Grid reference: SK 149829*

DOG FRIENDLINESS *Farmland, dogs should be kept on lead*

PARKING *Main Castleton pay car park by visitor centre*

PUBLIC TOILETS *At car park*

Castleton is the last settlement before the Hope Valley narrows and squeezes into the rocky ravine of Winnats. It's a bustling tourist town with a history evident back to Norman times, and a geology that has been responsible for many of its successes and most of its failures.

At Castleton the shales and gritstone of the Dark Peak and the limestone plateaux of the White Peak meet. Here countless generations of miners have dug their shafts and enlarged the natural caves which riddle the bedrock in search of precious ore. Here too, they built an ambitious road that eventually succumbed to the landslides of Mam Tor, the 'Shivering Mountain'. The castle keep is perched high upon an outcrop of limestone. It's one of the earliest stone-built castles in the country, built shortly after the Norman Conquest by William Peveril, William the Conqueror's illegitimate son.

Dramatic Cave Dale

The entrance to Cave Dale is narrow and dramatic. One minute you're in the village square, the next you've turned the corner and entered an awesome limestone ravine. Geologists used to think Cave Dale was a collapsed cavern, but current thinking places it as a valley carved by glaciers of the last ice age.

A little limestone path takes you through the ravine, climbing past cave entrances and over the tops of a wide system of subterranean passages, including those of the nearby Peak Cavern. The valley shallows and the next stretch of the journey is over high green fields enclosed by dry-stone walls. Mam Tor, the Shivering Mountain, dominates the view ahead and soon you look down on the crumbling tarmac of the ill-fated road, and the huge shale landslides that have plagued the valley for centuries.

The first Castleton cavern of the day is the fantastic and very popular Blue John Mine, high on the side of Mam Tor. It takes its name from the purple-blue fluorspar, unique to Castleton. The floodlights of the chambers show off the old river galleries with crystalline waterfalls, and a fascinating array of stalagmites and stalactites.

Trips

…nd the Blue John Mine a narrow path rakes across the steep limestone-studded slopes past Treak Cliff Cavern to the Speedwell Cavern, at the foot of the Winnats Pass. If you like boat trips, a visit to this cavern is a must. Here, lead miners excavated a level into the hill, through which they built a subterranean canal, 547yds (500m) long. This took them 11 years, but low yields and high costs forced the early closure of the mine. The fascinating boat trip takes you down the canal to a landing stage just short of the 'Bottomless Pit', named because the spoil thrown in by miners made no impression on its depth.

The last stretch takes you across the National Trust's Longcliffe Estate. Before retreating to Castleton, take one last look back up the valley, and across the limestone that was once a coral reef in a tropical lagoon.

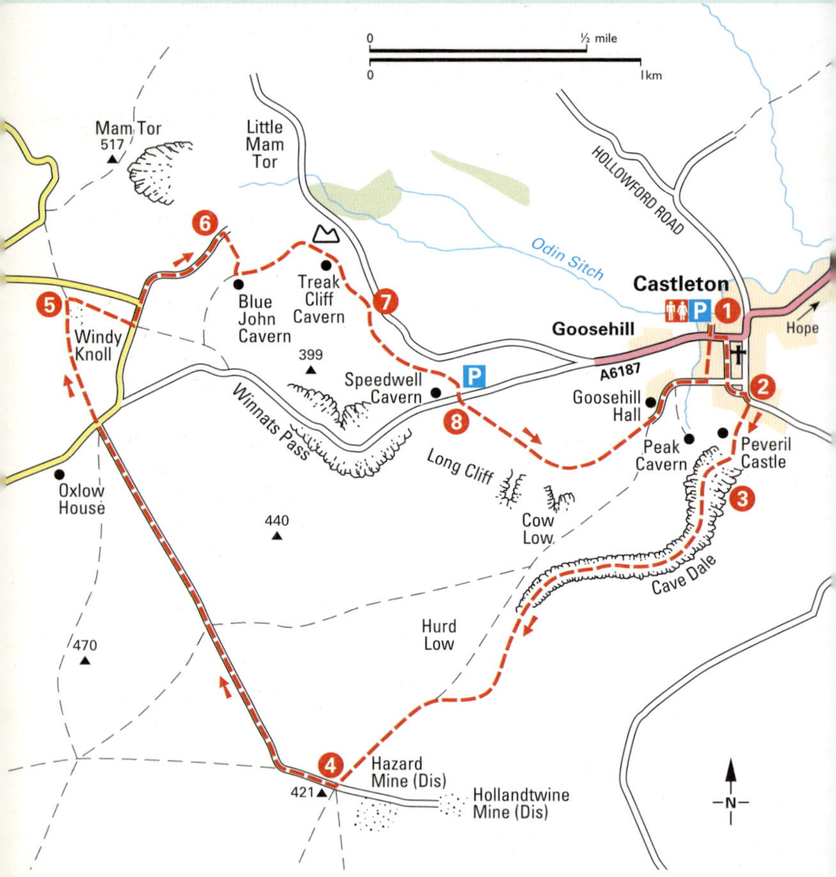

WALK 17 DIRECTIONS

❶ From the car park turn left to go down the main street and then turn right to walk along Castle Street, passing the church and the youth hostel on your way.

❷ On reaching the Market Place, turn left to Bar Gate, where a signpost points to Cave Dale. Through a gate, the path enters the limestone gorge with the ruined keep of Peveril Castle perched on the cliffs to the right.

WHAT TO LOOK FOR

Treak Cliff Cavern is one of the best places to see fossils. In the limestone you can study the remains of sea creatures that accumulated in the bed of a tropical sea 320 million years ago.

3 As you gain height the gorge shallows. Go through a gate in the dry-stone wall and follow the well-defined track across high pastureland. It passes through a gate in another wall before being joined by a path that has descended the grassy hillside on the right. The track divides soon after the junction. Take the left fork, which climbs uphill, slightly away from the wall on the right, to the top corner of the field. Go through the gate here and follow a short stretch of walled track to a crossroads of routes near the old Hazard Mine.

4 Turn right beyond the gate here to walk along a stony walled lane, which swings right to reach a minor road near Oxlow House Farm. Take the path across the road to the disused quarry on Windy Knoll.

5 At the quarry turn right on a grassy footpath to a minor road. After turning left to the next junction, take the old Mam Tor Road (straight ahead).

6 After 400yds (366m) turn right down the tarmac approach road to Blue John Cavern, then left by the ticket office. Go through the gate and trace the path as it crosses several fields. Beyond a gate the path arcs to the right, traversing the now steep grassy hillslopes. It passes Treak Cliff Cavern ticket office. Go left down the concrete steps by the ticket office, then right on a concrete path with handrails.

WHERE TO EAT AND DRINK

To complete your round-up of all the local places containing the word 'castle', try the 17th-century Castle in Castle Street, which serves food daily.

WHILE YOU'RE THERE

Besides the caverns seen en route, try and make time for Peveril Castle, looked after by English Heritage. Besides having a well-preserved Norman keep it offers wonderful views up Cave Dale and over the village.

7 Half-way down the steps, take the hillside path on the right, signposted 'Winnats Pass'. On the approach to Speedwell Cavern the path becomes indistinct, but there's an obvious stile straight ahead which will take you out on to the Winnats road.

8 A path on the far side of the road takes the route through the National Trust's Longcliff Estate. It roughly follows the line of a wall and veers left beneath the hill slopes of Cow Low to reach Goosehill Hall. Here, follow Goosehill (a lane), back into Castleton. Beyond Goosehill Bridge, turn left down a surfaced streamside path to the car park.

Overleaf: Mam Tor, Peak District National Park (Walk 17)

WALK 18

Marching Roads and Battlefields

Following the ancient roads over Win Hill to the Roman fort at Navio, via the site of an ancient battle.

DISTANCE *8.75 miles (14.1km)* **MINIMUM TIME** *5hrs*

ASCENT/GRADIENT *1,050ft (320m)* ▲▲▲ **LEVEL OF DIFFICULTY** +++

PATHS *Paths can be slippery after rain, quite a few stiles*

LANDSCAPE *Riverside pastureland and high peak*

SUGGESTED MAP *OS Explorer OL1 Dark Peak*

START/FINISH *Grid reference: SK 149829*

DOG FRIENDLINESS *Dogs on lead*

PARKING *Main Castleton pay car park*

PUBLIC TOILETS *At car park*

Leaving Castleton beneath Peveril Castle's Norman keep sets the scene for a walk through history. You're treading the same ground as Roman soldiers and Celtic and Saxon warriors before you. The walk takes you on to the hillside beyond the sycamores of the River Noe. As you amble across green pastures overlooking the Hope Valley, cast your imagination back to the darker days of AD 926. Down there in the valley below you, a furious tribal battle ended in victory for King Athelstan, grandson of Alfred the Great. He would soon become the first Saxon ruler of all England.

Navio – a Roman Fort

In one of those riverside fields the path comes across the earthwork remains of the Roman fort, Navio. Built in the time of Emperor Antoninus Pius, the fort stood at a junction of roads serving garrisons at Buxton, Glossop, and Templeborough. At its peak it would have sheltered over 500 soldiers. It remained occupied until the 4th century, controlling the rich mining area around the Peak. Many Roman relics found near the fort can be viewed at the Buxton Museum.

Win Hill looms large in your thoughts as you cross to the other side of the valley and climb towards it. As you're passing through the hamlet of Aston take a quick look at Aston Hall. Built in 1578, it has an unusual pedimented window with a weather-worn carved figure. The doorway is surrounded by Roman Doric columns and a four-centred arch.

Beyond the hall the climb begins in earnest up a stony track, then through bracken and grass hillside where Win Hill's rocky summit peeps out across the heathered ridge. A concrete trig point caps the rocks. And what a view to reward your efforts! Ladybower Reservoir's sinuous shorelines creep between dark spruce woods, while the gritstone tors of Kinder Scout, Derwent Edge, and Bleaklow fill the northern horizon, framed by the pyramidal Lose Hill.

There are several theories on how Win Hill got its name. The most likely one is that it derives from an earlier name, Wythinehull, which meant Willow Hill. The one some prefer though concerns two warlords, Edwin, the first Christian king of Northumbria, and Cuicholm, King of Wessex. Cuicholm murdered Lilla, Edwin's maidservant, and Edwin was looking for revenge. Cuicholm assembled his forces on Lose Hill, while his enemy camped on Win Hill. Edwin was victorious and thus his hill was named Win Hill. Now you follow Edwin down the hill, before continuing across the Hope Valley fields back to Castleton.

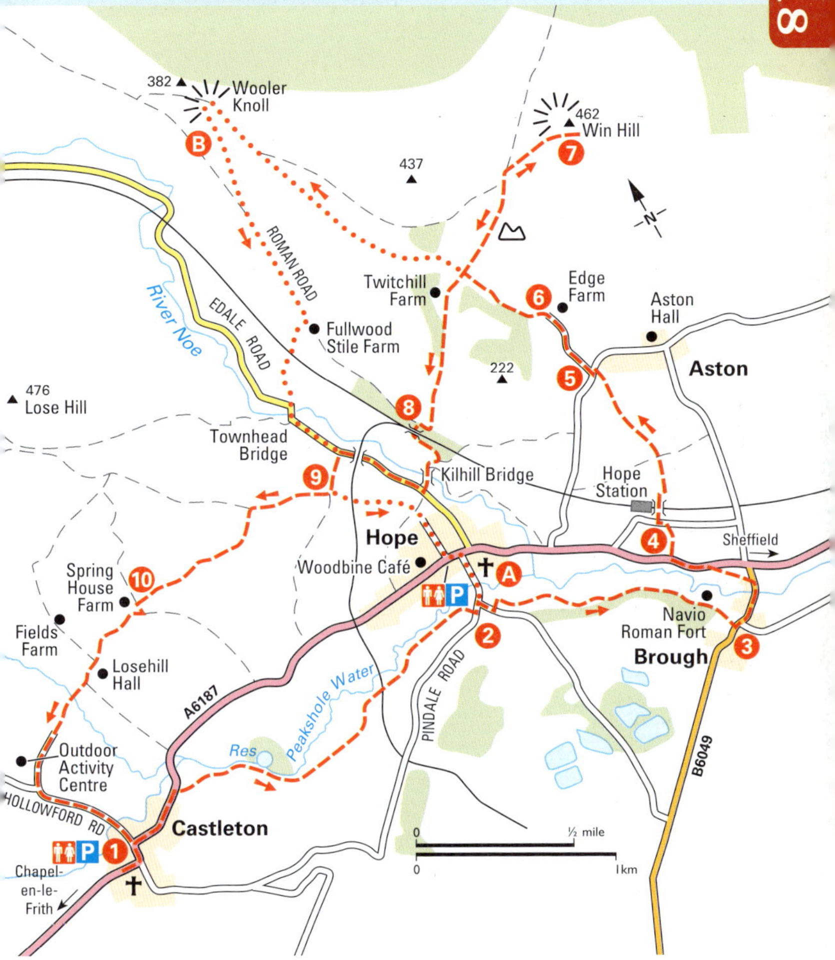

WALK 18 DIRECTIONS

1 Turn left out of the car park along the main street. At the far end of the village turn right on a walled stony lane and continue along a well-defined path accompanying Peakshole Water. Cross the railway with care and continue along the path to its end at Pindale Road.

2 Turn left here, then right at the next junction. After 200yds (183m), go over a stile by a gate on the left and follow the path running roughly parallel to the lane at first, then the River Noe, to reach the site of the Roman fort of Navio. Beyond the earthworks go over a stile in a fence and bear half right across another field to reach the B6049 road at Brough.

WHERE TO EAT AND DRINK

The Castle is a 17th-century coaching inn on Castle Street, Castleton. It serves Bass beer and good bar meals. Closer to hand you could seek out the popular Woodbine Café in Hope, which serves pies, bacon sandwiches and hot drinks.

3 Turn left through the village and cross the footbridge over the River Noe. Go left over a stile and head north-west to the A6187. Cross over and turn left along the road for 200yds (183m) to a small gate just beyond a cottage. Follow the hedge and dyke on the right to pass to the right of some houses.

4 Turn left along the lane heading towards the railway station, then go right along a narrow path, which leads to a footbridge over the line. Cross the bridge and turn right at its far end, then left through a gate to cross yet more fields, this time keeping the fence on your right.

WHILE YOU'RE THERE

If you're here on August Bank Holiday Monday you should visit the Hope Agricultural Show and sheepdog trials.

5 When you reach Aston turn left along the road, then almost immediately turn right along a narrow, surfaced lane, signposted 'Win Hill and Hope Cross'.

6 Beyond Edge Farm an unsurfaced track on the left takes the route along the top edge of some woods to a path junction above Twitchill Farm. Now climb right on a well-used path to Win Hill's summit.

7 From the summit retrace your steps back to the junction above Twitchill Farm. This time descend left past the farm on the surfaced drive to the railway.

8 Turn left under the railway tunnel for the lane via Kilhill Bridge to Edale Road. Turn right along the road, under the railway bridge, then turn left by a red postbox in a wall on a field path.

9 By the outbuildings of a cottage, turn right on a path climbing towards Lose Hill. Take the left fork at a junction of paths to follow a waymarked route signposted to Castleton westwards to Spring House Farm.

10 In front of the farm, turn right to walk along a track behind Losehill Hall. Where the lane swings left, leave it to follow a cross-field path, which joins a rough lane. After passing the outdoor centre, turn left along Hollowford Road into Castleton.

WHAT TO LOOK OUT FOR

Often you can see a change in the dry-stone walls. Those in the valley are made from paler limestone, while those on the Win Hill slopes are of the darker gritstone. The walls were mostly built between 1780 and 1820, when enclosure of upland areas was taking place at a prolific rate. Although expensive to build and repair, they're are now considered to be an integral part of the Peakland landscape.

Navio and Aston from Hope

A shorter route misses out the climb to the summit of Win Hill, but still takes in the fine views.

See map and information panel for Walk 18

DISTANCE *5 miles (8km)* **MINIMUM TIME** *3hrs*

ASCENT/GRADIENT *754ft (230m)* ▲▲▲ **LEVEL OF DIFFICULTY** +++

START/FINISH *Grid reference: SK 172835*

PARKING *Hope pay car park*

PUBLIC TOILETS *At car park*

WALK 19 DIRECTIONS (Walk 18 option)

This is a shorter version of Walk 18 but you will still enjoy the good views on a clear day by ascending as far as Twitchill Farm, but miss out the climb to the summit of Win Hill.

From the car park at Hope, turn right along the Main Street, then right again up Pindale Road by St Peter's Church (Point A).

The squat, broad spired tower of the church dates back to the 14th century. The font is Norman, the only thing remaining from the original 13th-century building, while the well-preserved oak pulpit was carved in 1652.

On reaching the T-junction at Point 2, follow Walk 18 across the fields to Navio Roman Fort, then uphill past Aston to Point 6, above Twitchill Farm. This time continue along the track, raking up the side of the hill to Wooler Knoll (Point B), where you get a good view over the Woodlands Valley without having to complete the steep climb.

At the top, turn left on to the ridge track for 200yds (183m), then left down an unsignposted bridleway track, which descends to the old Roman road. Follow this ancient route past Fullwood Stile Farm and continue along the lane to Townhead Bridge.

Follow Edale Road southwards to a signposted path on the right – the spot is highlighted by a red postbox in the wall (Point 9). The path follows the field to some farm outbuildings.

Once over the stile by the buildings turn left on a track passing to the left of a cottage. Go over the stile straight ahead and follow the path across the bridge over a railway cutting. Continue along a path across the fields towards Hope, passing some caravans. The path reaches a road by the village school. Go straight ahead into a small housing estate and along the ginnel on the left. This leads the route back into Hope's village centre.

WALK 20

Climbers' Gritstone on the Eastern Edges

Walking along the Froggatt, Curbar and White edges – the proving ground for a new breed of rock climber.

DISTANCE *8.75 miles (14.1km)* **MINIMUM TIME** *4hrs*

ASCENT/GRADIENT *525ft (160m)* ▲▲▲ **LEVEL OF DIFFICULTY** +++

PATHS *Good paths and tracks, a few stiles*

LANDSCAPE *Heather moor and gritstone cliffs*

SUGGESTED MAP *OS Explorer OL24 White Peak*

START/FINISH *Grid reference: SK 255776*

DOG FRIENDLINESS *Dogs on lead*

PARKING *Hay Wood National Trust pay car park*

PUBLIC TOILETS *None on route*

WALK 20 DIRECTIONS

Gritstone is soluble rock, and so quickly loses its edges, leaving few natural handholds for climbers. W P Hasket Smith, the 'inventor' of rock climbing, said in his book, *Climbing in the British Isles* (1894), 'Millstone grit assumes strange grotesque forms, and when it does offer a climb, ends it off abruptly'. He conceded that it did have pleasing problems. But in the 1950s working class, urban pioneers such as Joe Brown, armed with makeshift gear like their mothers' clothes lines, found new ways to tackle the rocks. Joe and fellow plumber Don Whillans, introduced the use of 'nuts' for protection, and the 'handjam', where the climber puts his outstretched hand into a narrow cleft in the rocks, then clenches it into a fist. This jams the hand in, allowing the whole weight of the body to be supported.

And with these developments climbing came to Derbyshire on a much larger scale. Froggatt and Curbar edges, like those of Stanage to the north, are high on the priority list for most northern climbers, and for much of today's walk you'll see them, clinging precariously to the rock face or standing at the foot of the crag with their modern ironmongery and coloured ropes.

From the car park in Hay Wood, turn right (north) along the path towards the Longshaw Estate. Go right through a small gate in the wall to follow a faint path diagonally across fields to The Grouse Inn, which is always in view. From the inn, follow the road northwards for 400yds (366m) to take the second bridleway on the right past White Edge Lodge to the road junction on Totley Moss. Turn right for a few paces, then go over a stile onto a fence-side path heading south across the moors.

After passing copses of pine, the path heads south over White Edge Moor, passing through a gap in a stone cross wall before continuing to the Hurkling Stones on the northern end of White Edge.

WHAT TO LOOK OUT FOR

On the heather moors and edges, look out for birds of prey like the peregrine falcon or the merlin. You may see emperor moths fluttering about in the heather. They have red, gold and grey wings with black eyes. Their caterpillars are bright green and black. Northern oak eggar moths are also found hereabouts.

The expansive moorland to the east is covered with heather and ling – this is part of a wildlife sanctuary extending all the way into Yorkshire. To the west the hill slopes fall away to the birch and rowan fringed rocks of Froggatt Edge.

Beyond the trig point on White Edge the path passes above some enclosed rough pastures, then continues as a narrow path descending on the west slopes of the now grassy moor.

The path reaches a country lane, north-west of its junction with the A621. Cross the lane to a gate on the other side. Through the gate a wide track traverses the heather fields of Eaglestone Flat. To the left across birch woods you'll see the cliffs of Gardom's Edge and, in the valley, the park-like grounds of Chatsworth.

WHILE YOU'RE THERE

Longshaw Estate was a shooting estate, owned by the Duke of Rutland until 1927. It includes the lodge (closed to the public), planned grounds, woodland and the surrounding grouse moors. In the late 1920s, when the estate came on the market, a charity which included local rambling clubs, was set up to buy the land. It was then donated to the National Trust, who keep it open for the public. The woodland is noted for its varied bird-life.

The track comes to Wellington's Monument, which was erected in 1866 to commemorate the great British General. In the distance you can just see the monument to that other great warrior of those times, Admiral Lord Nelson.

WHERE TO EAT AND DRINK

The Grouse Inn, a short way from the car park, at Hay Wood, serves food. There's a café at Longshaw Estate Visitor Centre.

Follow the track round to the right, before taking the right fork past the Eagle Stone. In bygone days the young men of Baslow used to demonstrate their manliness by climbing this rock.

The path continues across the lane at Curbar Gap and on to the Curbar Edge path. Once through the first gate you can see the Derwent Valley villages dotted among the walled pastures and woods, and with the rolling hills of the Hope Valley beyond.

Although there is a wide track about 30yds (27m) from the edge, the best route stays closer to the cliff top. This route affords spectacular views as it veers right above Froggatt Edge. There's a diversion on the right here to visit a Bronze Age circle. After rejoining the main path, follow it to a roadside kissing gate.

Turn right up the road, then left on a path to Hay Wood car park.

Overleaf: Curbar Edge, Peak District National Park (Walk 20)

WALK 21

On the Edge at Stanage

Skirting the gritstone cliffs which line Sheffield's moorland edge.

DISTANCE *9 miles (14.5km)* **MINIMUM TIME** *5hrs 30min*
ASCENT/GRADIENT *1,150ft (350m)* ▲▲▲ **LEVEL OF DIFFICULTY** +++
PATHS *Well-defined paths and tracks, a few stiles*
LANDSCAPE *Gritstone and heather moorland*
SUGGESTED MAP *OS Explorer OL1 Dark Peak*
START/FINISH *Grid reference: SK 232814*
DOG FRIENDLINESS *Dogs should be kept on lead*
PARKING *Hathersage car park*
PUBLIC TOILETS *At car park, and on lane above North Lees*

From Moscar to Baslow a line of dark cliffs cap the heather moors east of the Derwent Valley. Defoe, ever the scourge of mountain scenery, called it a vast extended moor or waste in which strangers would be obliged to take guides or lose their way. Later Emily Brontë came here to visit her friend Ellen Nussey, the wife of the local vicar. Emily would have found the place much more acceptable, and not unlike her home at Haworth.

Early Climbers

In the 1890s, the climber, J W Putrell turned to the highest of these cliffs, Stanage Edge, and pioneered several gully routes. Others would follow and today Stanage and its neighbouring 'edges' are one of the most popular climbing venues in Britain. But Stanage is a great place for walkers too, for they can stride out on firm skyline paths with Yorkshire on one side and Derbyshire on the other. High car parks mean that you can walk Stanage without much ascent, but it is more rewarding to work for your fun, so instead you start the route at Hathersage.

The Eyres of Hathersage

Hathersage is a neat village by the banks of the River Derwent. The route starts gently on Baulk Lane and passes the cricket ground on its way through the little valley of Hood Brook. Gradients steepen and the route comes across the 16th-century castellated manor of North Lees Hall, the inspiration for Thornfield Hall, Mr Rochester's home in *Jane Eyre*. The Eyre family did exist in real life. They were Roman Catholics who lived in the hall until the 17th century, when a narrow-minded Protestant community drove them out. The remains of a chapel, built in 1685, only to be destroyed three years later, can still be seen in the grounds.

Above the hall the route climbs on to the moors and a paved causey track known as Jacob's Ladder takes it to the top of the cliffs. The cliff-edge path to High Neb and Crow Chin is an absolute delight, and the views from it are extensive, taking in a good deal of the Derwent and Hope valleys, Mam Tor and Kinder Scout. It may seem strange to descend to the foot of the cliffs, but the lost height doesn't amount to much and you can now view them from the perspective of the climber.

After rejoining the edge, the path passes above Robin Hood's Cave, where the legendary outlaw perhaps hid from the Sheriff of Nottingham, to reach the high road and climbers' car park. Now there is just Higger Tor to do. The rocky knoll surrounded by an ocean of heather makes a fine finale, one last lofty perch before the descent back to Hathersage.

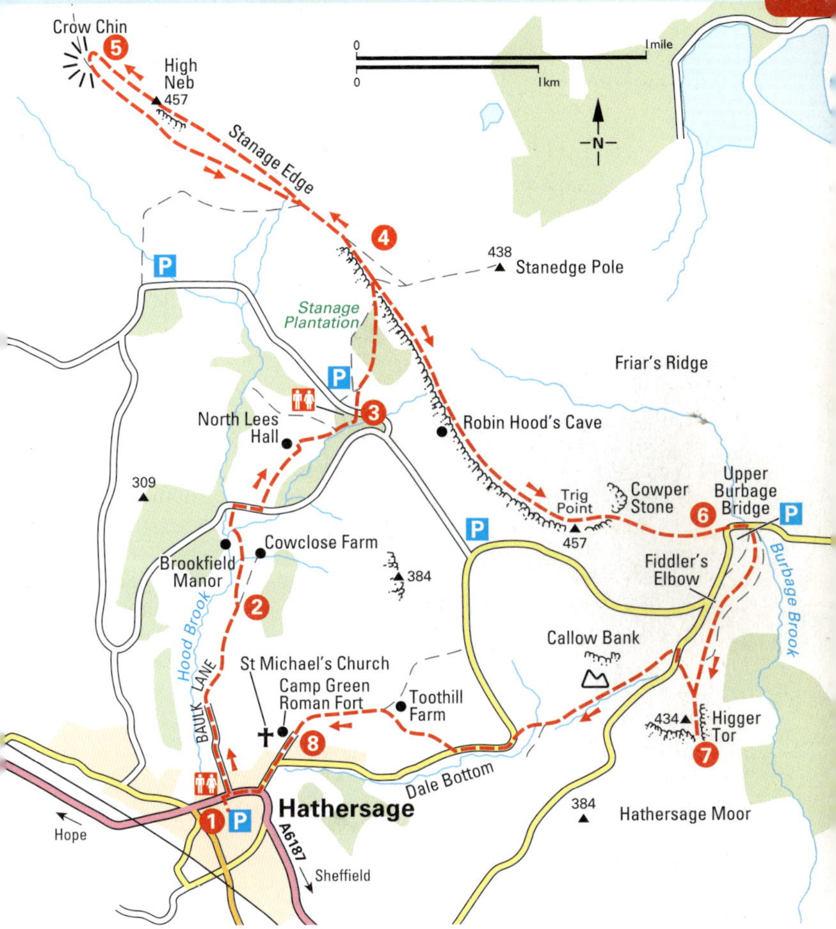

WALK 21 DIRECTIONS

1 At the car park in Hathersage, take the path in the corner past the Methodist church to Main Road. Turn right, cross over, then turn left in Baulk Lane. The lane climbs steadily north, passing the cricket ground. Beyond the buildings it becomes an unsurfaced track.

2 Just short of Cowclose Farm take the signposted left fork, which passes to the right of Brookfield Manor to reach a country lane. Turn right here, then left along a drive to North Lees Hall. After rounding the hall, turn right, climbing some steps that cut the corner to another track. This crosses hillside pastures before continuing through woodland.

3 A stepped path on the left makes a short cut to a roadside toilet block and mountain rescue post. Cross the road for a grassy path heading for the rocks of Stanage Edge. After 200yds (183m) you join the path from the nearby car park. A paved path now climbs through Stanage Plantation before arcing left to the cliff top and turning left.

4 Follow the firm edge-top path north-westwards to see the impressive summit of High Neb and Crow Chin.

WHILE YOU'RE THERE

Take a look round the parish Church of St Michael, which you pass on the hillsides above the village. It dates back to the 14th century, though the Perpendicular tower and its spire are 100 years younger. The stained-glass east window comes from the doomed church of Derwent before it was submerged beneath the rising waters of Ladybower Reservoir. In the churchyard a particularly long grave is claimed to be that of Robin Hood's henchman, Little John.

5 When you reach Crow Chin, where the edge veers north, descend to a lower path that doubles back beneath the cliffs. This eventually joins a track from the right, which returns the route to the top of the cliffs. Continue walking towards the south-east along the edge to the bouldery east summit (marked on Ordnance Survey maps by a spot height of 457m), whose rocks are capped by a concrete trig point.

6 The track continues to the road at Upper Burbage Bridge. Proceed left along the road for about 150yds (137m), then turn right by the car park, taking the the higher of the two paths which head south to the lofty heights of the summit of Higger Tor.

WHAT TO LOOK FOR

Beneath the cliffs of Stanage Edge you'll see piles of old millstones and grindstones, some intact, and some incomplete. They are the abandoned relics of an industry that supplied the flourishing steelworks of Sheffield and local corn mills. French imports, which were both cheaper and better, and the coming of the roller mills saw the decline of the industry by the 1860s.

7 From the rocky top, double back (roughly north of north-west) on a path to the Fiddler's Elbow road. Slightly uphill along the road take the path on the left. This descends Callow Bank to reach a walled track leading down to the Dale Bottom road. Follow the road for 300yds (274m) to a track on the right that traverses the hill slopes to Toothill Farm. Turn left by the farmhouse on a drive that soon joins a tarred lane taking the route down to Hathersage's impressively spired church and the Roman fort of Camp Green.

8 Turn right down School Lane to reach Main Road, which leads you back into the centre of Hathersage. Go left before the toilets to reach the car park.

WHERE TO EAT AND DRINK

The Scotsman's Pack, on School Lane, Hathersage, is an old coaching inn serving Burtonwood beers and excellent bar meals. It has outside seating by a tinkling stream. There's often a snack van on the car park at Upper Burbage Bridge.

From Dark to White

On conical Chrome Hill the dramatic landscape changes, from limestone to gritstone.

DISTANCE *7.5 miles (12.1km)* **MINIMUM TIME** *4hrs 30min*

ASCENT/GRADIENT *980ft (300m)* ▲▲▲ **LEVEL OF DIFFICULTY** +++

PATHS *Good paths except for ones between Hollinsclough and Brand End, can be slippery after rain, lots of stiles*

LANDSCAPE *Gritstone moors and cloughs with limestone hills*

SUGGESTED MAP *OS Explorer OL24 White Peak*

START/FINISH *Grid reference: SK 034697*

DOG FRIENDLINESS *Farmland, dogs should be kept under close control*

PARKING *Axe Edge car park*

PUBLIC TOILETS *None on route*

When you stand on Axe Edge, you are standing on the Pennine watershed. Just to prove it, you can see five rivers, the Goyt, the Dane, the Dove, the Wye and the Manifold, each going their separate ways towards the Irish and North seas from near here. You are 1,660ft (506m) above sea level on one of the wildest gritstone moors of the Dark Peak, but when you look east you're looking across to the White Peak valley of the Dove. It is a fascinating view with several rocky hills vying for your attention. One angular one stands out from all the rest – that is Chrome Hill, and it is the high point of the day.

A pleasant, narrow lane takes the walk deep down into the valley, and soon you are following an old green road beneath Leap Edge. If you can hear buzzing noises it is not your ears: it is either that of racing cars roaring around the track on the nearby High Edge Raceway or model aeroplanes soaring on the thermals of the hillside.

The Dragon's Back

Chrome Hill hides behind Hollins Hill for a while, but once you've climbed round the limestone knoll of Tor Rock you see it again rearing up into the sky. It's hard to believe, but Chrome Hill and its neighbours are the remains of coral reefs formed over 320 million years ago, when Derbyshire lay under a warm tropical sea near the equator. Arches and caves, spires and fissures, have been carved out of the coral, creating this fascinating peak. You can see why it's sometimes known as the Dragon's Back.

There's a steep downhill section to do before the climb, then the footpath seems to take a timid line along the west side. Just as you think you've missed the summit path, the one you're on turns left and climbs for the sky. The path doesn't always keep to the crest, but avoids mild scrambles by plotting a devious course round the top rocks. Experienced walkers with a head for heights may well prefer to 'ride the dragon's back'.

From the top, Parkhouse Hill captures your attention. It's not unlike Chrome Hill, but it hasn't got a path yet. So our route descends to the little road at its foot, and takes a good look before following a pleasant farm track into Hollinsclough. On summer Sundays they serve tea and cakes in the village hall, a nice break before heading back across Hollinsclough Rake. The path comes to this shady corner between three hills and by the confluence of two brooks. There's a fine old packhorse bridge to cross, and the cobbled Leycote track takes you uphill to the next field path. The paths round here are not well used, but they're pretty ones, through woodland and across fields of wild flowers. Farm tracks and a narrow country lane make the last bit of this journey easy.

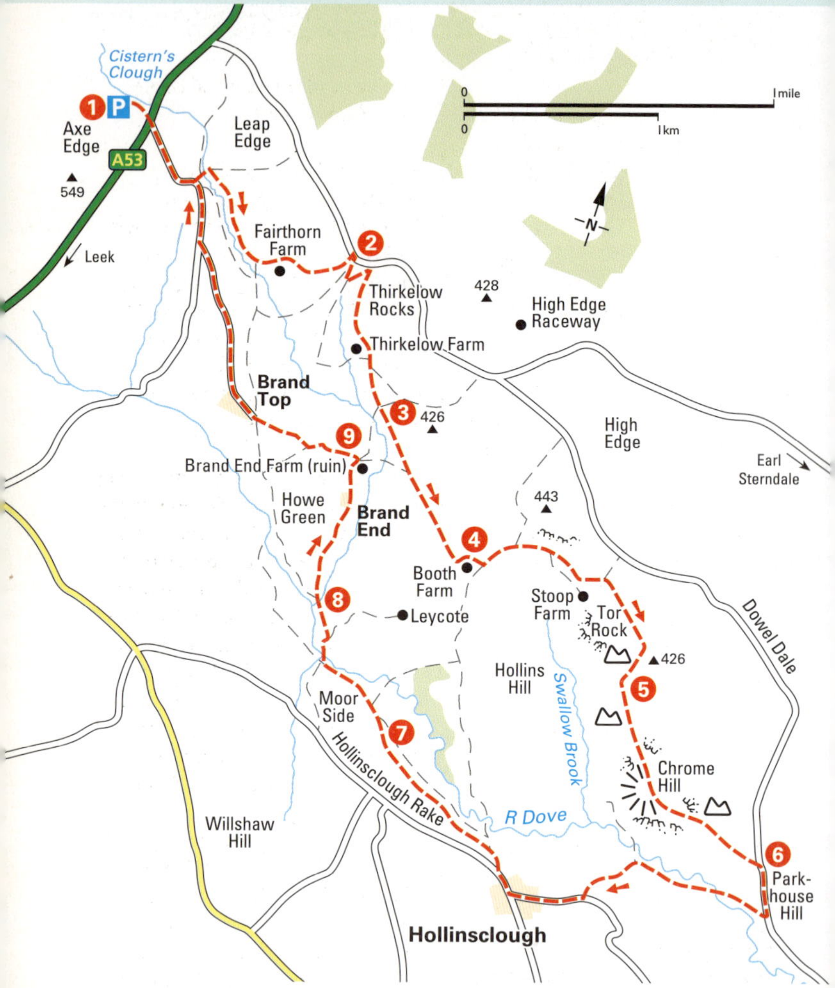

WALK 22 DIRECTIONS

1 From the car park cross the main road and descend the lane opposite. At the first right-hand bend turn left to take the left of two farm tracks, descending to cross the Cistern's Clough bridge heading for Fairthorn Farm. Past the house swing left on the drive up to the road at Thirkelow Rocks.

2 Turn right along the road for 200yds (183m), then take the

WHAT TO LOOK OUT FOR

The elements have carved out arches and caves in the Carboniferous limestone, making Chrome Hill a fascinating place for geologists. You may spot fossils in the stones of the limestone walls. Limestone-loving plants such as field scabious and harebells will be a common sight along the walk, as will the skylark, lapwing and wheatear.

farm track on the right, heading south past Thirkelow Farm. Take the right fork into the clough.

3 Where the track ends, veer slightly right to the waymarking posts highlighting a duckboard bridge and the continuing route towards Booth Farm.

4 Keep to the left of the farm and go over some steps in the wall ahead. After crossing a small field, turn left along the farm road, then fork right for Stoop Farm. Turn left along a waymarked field path, bypassing the farmhouse and climbing to a footpath intersection at the top wall. Take the path signposted 'Glutton Bridge via Chrome Hill'.

5 Drop down to a stile and follow a wallside path that eventually climbs left to the crest before continuing over the summit, and descending to the

WHERE TO EAT AND DRINK

On Sundays from May to August, tea and cakes are served in the village hall at Hollinsclough. The nearest pub is the Quiet Woman at Earl Sterndale, an old-fashioned, village local serving bar snacks. Its sign depicts a headless woman – supposedly the fate of the over-talkative wife of a former landlord!

WHILE YOU'RE THERE

Nearby East Sterndale is worth a visit. It is a charming village, huddled round a small green. The 19th-century St Michael's Church was bombed in the Second World War, the only church in Derbyshire to suffer such a fate. It was restored in 1952, and still has its original Saxon font intact.

lane beneath the conical shape of Parkhouse Hill.

6 Turn right to walk along the lane, then right again to follow a farm track. Take the left fork to reach a surfaced road, just short of Hollinsclough. Walk through the village, going right at the junction, then cross over a stile on the right. Take the higher left fork that traverses Hollinsclough Rake.

7 On reaching the green zig-zag track at Moor Side, descend right to pass a ruin and continue up a narrow valley. Cross the stream and go over the stile to reach an old packhorse bridge. Across the bridge take a stony track climbing towards the farm buildings at Leycote. On a sharp right-hand bend go left through a gate and follow a narrow path heading north-west into a wooded clough.

8 Follow the path across the simple slab bridge and climb up through the bracken towards Brand End. Go right at the fork at the top. The path becomes a more obvious track, passing Brand End Cottage and descending to the ruins of Brand End Farm.

9 Turn left up the bank by a wall here, passing to the left of another farm. Turn left along a farm track to Brand Top. Here the road leads you back to Axe Edge.

WALK 23

Ghosts of Miller's Dale

The rural serenity of modern Miller's Dale belies its early role in the Industrial Revolution.

DISTANCE *6 miles (9.7km)* **MINIMUM TIME** *4hrs*

ASCENT/GRADIENT *690ft (210m)* ▲▲▲ **LEVEL OF DIFFICULTY** +++

PATHS *Generally well-defined paths and tracks, path in Water-cum-Jolly Dale liable to flooding, quite a few stiles*

LANDSCAPE *Limestone dales*

SUGGESTED MAP *OS Explorer OL24 White Peak*

START/FINISH *Grid reference: SK 154743*

DOG FRIENDLINESS *Dogs on lead in nature reserves and around livestock in fields*

PARKING *Tideswell Dale pay car park*

PUBLIC TOILETS *At car park*

It's all quiet in Miller's Dale these days, but it wasn't always so. Many early industrialists wanted to build their cotton mills in the countryside, far away from the marauding Luddites of the city. The Wye and its tributaries had the power to work these mills. The railway followed, and that brought more industry with it. And so little Miller's Dale and its neighbours joined the Industrial Revolution.

The walk starts in Tideswell Dale. Nowadays it's choked with thickets and herbs but they hide a history of quarrying and mining. Here the miners wanted basalt, a dark, hard igneous rock that was used for road building.

Cruelty at the Mill

Litton Mill has now been converted into comfortable flats and apartments, but it still holds dark secrets of a previous life. *The Memoirs of Robert Blincoe*, written in 1863, tells of mill owner Ellis Needham's cruelty to child apprentices, who were often shipped in from the poorhouses of London. Many of the children died and were buried in the churchyards of Tideswell and Taddington. It is said that ghosts of some of the apprentices still make appearances in or around the mill.

The walk emerges into Water-cum-Jolly Dale. At first the river is lined by mudbanks thick with rushes and common horsetail. It's popular with wildfowl. The river widens out and, at the same time, impressive limestone cliffs squeeze the path. The river's widening is artificial, a result of it being controlled to form a head of water for the downstream mill.

Round the next corner is Cressbrook Mill, built by Sir Richard Arkwright, but taken over by William Newton. Newton also employed child labour but was said to have treated them well. The rooftop bell tower would have peeled to beckon the apprentices, who lived next door, to the works. Like Litton this impressive Georgian mill was allowed to moulder, but has now been restored as flats. The walk leaves the banks of the Wye at Cressbrook to take in pretty Cressbrook Dale. In this nature reserve you'll see lily-of-the-valley, wild garlic and bloody cranesbill; you should also see bee and fragrant orchids. Just as you think you've found your true rural retreat you'll climb to the rim of the dale, look across it and see the grassed-over spoil heaps of lead mines. Finally, the ancient strip fields of Litton form a picturesque mosaic of pasture and dry-stone wall on the return to Tideswell Dale.

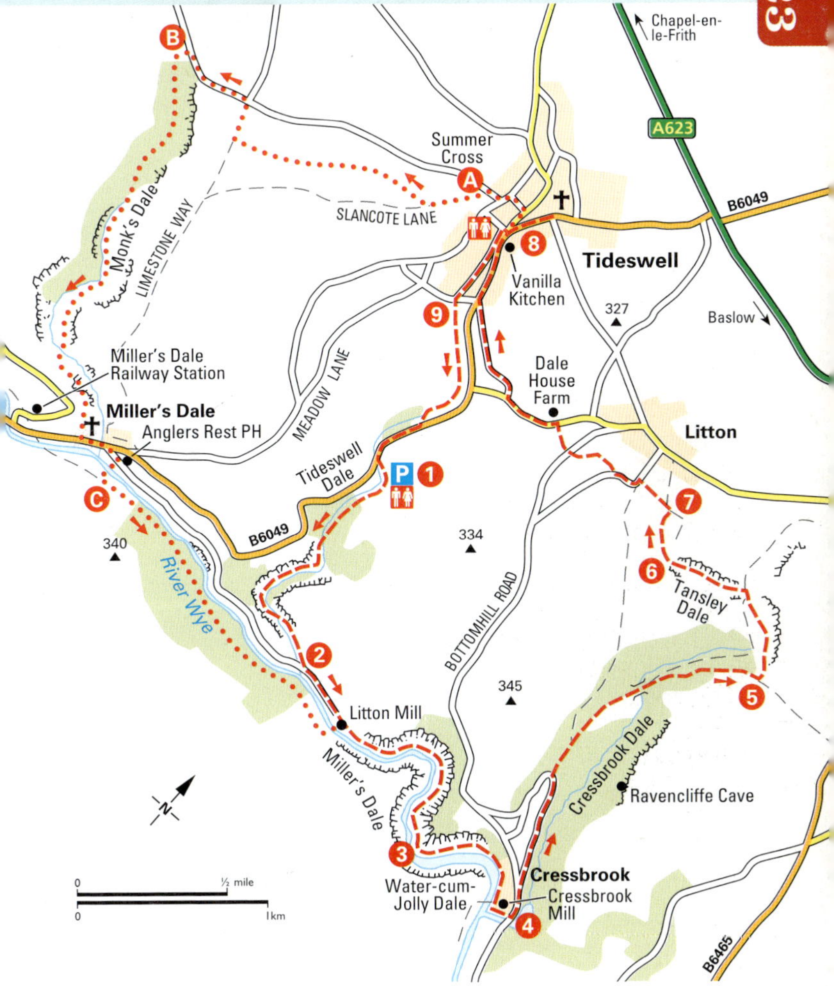

WALK 23 DIRECTIONS

1 Follow the path southwards from beside the car park's toilet block into Tideswell Dale, taking the right-hand fork to cross over the little bridge.

2 On entering Miller's Dale, go left along the tarmac lane and continue to Litton Mill. Go through the gateposts on to a concessionary path through the mill yard. Beyond the mill, the path follows the River Wye, as it meanders through the tight, steep-sided dale.

3 The river widens out in Water-cum-Jolly Dale and the path, liable to flooding here, traces a wall of limestone cliffs before reaching Cressbrook. Do not cross the bridge on the right, but turn left to pass in front of Cressbrook Mill and out on to the road.

4 Turn left along the road, then take the right fork which climbs steadily into Cressbrook Dale. Where the road doubles back uphill leave it for a track going straight ahead into the woods. Beyond a gate the track becomes a narrow path that emerges in a clearing high above the stream. Follow it downhill to a footbridge over the stream, then take the right fork path, which climbs high up the valley side to a stile in the top wall.

WHILE YOU'RE THERE

Miller's Dale Railway Station is a fascinating old site with a good deal of information on the railway, the wildlife and the walking. The station was built in 1863 for the Midland Railway. It was an important junction for the Buxton branch line, and in 1904 it was enlarged to provide a second platform and a second viaduct across the River Wye. The line went under the Beeching axe in 1967 and wild flowers now line the sides of the trackbed.

5 Don't cross the stile, take the downhill path to the dale bottom, where there's a junction of paths. The one wanted here recrosses the stream on stepping stones, and climbs into Tansley Dale.

6 The path turns right at the top of the dale, and follows a tumbledown wall before crossing it on a step stile. Head for a wall corner in the next field, then veer right through a narrow enclosure to reach a walled track just south of Litton village.

WHAT TO LOOK OUT FOR

Cressbrook Dale is part of the Derbyshire Dales National Nature Reserve. On the limestone grassland you may see orchids, cranesbill, mountain pansy, globeflower and spring sandwort. One of the many limestone-loving plants is the Nottingham catchfly (Silene nutans). The ragged white flowers roll back in daytime, but are fragrant at night. Small insects are caught on the sticky stalks but in this case nature is being wasteful, for they're never devoured by the plant.

7 Turn left along the track, which comes out onto a country lane at the crown of a sharp bend. Keep straight on down the lane but leave it at the next bend for a well-defined cross-field path to Bottomhill Road. Across the road, a further field path descends to a road at Dale House Farm. Turn left along the pavement, then right on a narrow lane marked 'unsuitable for motor traffic', into Tideswell.

8 After looking around the village head south down the main street, then right on to Gordon Road, which then heads south.

9 Where this ends, continue down the stony track ahead, which runs parallel with the main road. At the far end, take the gated footpath on the left, down to the road into Tideswell Dale. Turn right along the road, back to the car park.

WHERE TO EAT AND DRINK

The Anglers Rest, an atmospheric pub, at Miller's Dale and the Vanilla Kitchen café in Tideswell are both recommended for their warm welcome to weary walkers.

An Extension into Monk's Dale

If the weather is dry, take this tour round another secluded limestone dale.

See map and information panel for Walk 23

DISTANCE *8.5 miles (13.7km)* **MINIMUM TIME** *5hrs*
ASCENT/GRADIENT *790ft (240m)* ▲▲▲ **LEVEL OF DIFFICULTY** +++

WALK 24 DIRECTIONS (Walk 23 option)

Monk's Dale is a pleasant side valley, forming the bottom end of a much longer dale which stretches north from the River Wye under a variety of pseudonyms as far as Peak Forest. It's usually much quieter than its more famous neighbour.

Follow Walk 23 into Tideswell (Point 8). After visiting the church, head back into the village centre, turn right down Parke Road and left at Sherwood Road. Turn right up Summer Cross for a few paces, then left on to the track known as Slancote Lane (Point A) south-west away from the village.

After 400yds (366m) take the waymarked path over a stone stile by a gate on the right. The field path follows the wall westwards across numerous fields and the end of a farm track. Finally, it descends one large field before climbing up to a walled track used by the Limestone Way.

There is a quick way back into Miller's Dale by turning left along this track – an advisable alternative after rainy periods, for Monk's Dale can get flooded and even more slippery than usual. Otherwise, turn right, then left along the lane into Monk's Dale (Point B).

Head southward now, down Monk's Dale, across a field at first then on a slippery limestone footpath through the woods. The narrow path emerges to climb the limestone dale sides before descending again to cross a footbridge over the stream. From here climb up the opposite side of the dale to a gate, beyond which a stepped footpath descends into Miller's Dale by its church. Turn left along the surfaced lane opposite until you reach The Anglers Rest pub, then turn right across two footbridges to the south side of the dale, before climbing to the old railway, now part of the Monsal Trail (Point C).

Turn left along the railway trackbed, then, after a bridge, descend left on the footpath signposted to Litton Mill. After recrossing the Wye, turn left along the lane and then right to walk along the Tideswell Dale path, back to the car park.

WALK 25

Chatsworth House – The Palace of the Peak

A relatively easy walk through the qrandiose grounds of one of England's loveliest stately homes.

DISTANCE *4.5 miles (7.2km)* **MINIMUM TIME** *2hrs 30min*

ASCENT/GRADIENT *400ft (122m)* ▲▲▲ **LEVEL OF DIFFICULTY** +++

PATHS *Good paths and tracks, a couple of stiles*

LANDSCAPE *Parkland and low afforested hills*

SUGGESTED MAP *OS Explorer OL24 White Peak*

START/FINISH *Grid reference: SK 258722*

DOG FRIENDLINESS *Dogs on lead in Chatsworth Park*

PARKING *Pay car park at Nether End, Baslow*

PUBLIC TOILETS *At car park*

WALK 25 DIRECTIONS

There are few more magnificent buildings in Britain than Chatsworth House and its splendid gardens. On his visit in 1726, Daniel Defoe wrote that he was astonished that 'so noble and magnificent a palace' should be built in such a harsh, out of the way situation.

This short walk from Baslow allows you to walk dryshod with stout shoes, and to visit the house without putting mud on the carpet. Having taken in the splendour you set off on a climb through the woods to see a lake, some crags and a wonderful view of the Derwent Valley.

Turn right out of the car park at Baslow and go over the bridge, then right again, along a lane heading south between the banks of Bar Brook and some charming little cottages. At the lane end go through an unusual kissing gate and follow the wide path across the lawned parklands of Chatsworth. Go past a cricket green to reach Queen Mary's Bower, a favoured spot of Mary, Queen of Scots, when she was imprisoned at Chatsworth by of the Earl of Shrewsbury in 1570.

Beyond the Bower the route reaches a decorative three-arched bridge over the River Derwent. From here you get one of the classic views of Chatsworth House, with the magnificent building's reflections rippling in the slow-moving waters of the Derwent River.

Turn left along the lane at the nearside of the bridge to reach the main entrance of the great mansion. The first Chatsworth House was completed in 1555 for Bess of Hardwick, a wealthy widow, and her new and equally wealthy husband, William Cavendish, who had helped Henry VIII dissolve the monasteries. Years later, Bess's grandson, William Cavendish, was made the first Duke of Devonshire and decided that Chatsworth wasn't grand enough for a Duke. So he pulled the old house down, replacing it with the present one between 1686 and 1708. In the 1820s the 6th Duke added the North Wing and invited the landscape architect 'Capability' Brown to design and landscape the gardens.

Walk uphill past the House and cafeteria and go through a gate by a cattle grid before taking the right fork, which arcs right, passing close to the farm. A path through the woods on the left, signposted to the Dell, cuts a corner to reach another surfaced road. Turn left along the road, which rounds the Hunting Tower, all that remains of the original Elizabethan mansion. The cannon outside the tower came from one of the battleships that fought in the Battle of Trafalgar.

Follow the road as it doubles back up the hillside on a detour to see the impressive Emperor Lake. The lake was constructed simply to supply a head of water for the Chatsworth Fountain.

WHAT TO LOOK OUT FOR

You can't really miss Chatsworth House, open from March to October. The magnificently decorated interior includes the Sculpture Gallery, which houses a large collection of classical and modern works collected by successive Dukes; and a library containing one of the finest private collections of books and prints in the world.

Return to the Hunting Tower, but this time take the metalled track heading north through conifers. At a junction of tracks with some huge barns to the right, go straight ahead to a gate at the edge of the woods. Turn left along the nearside of the perimeter wall, then go over it on a ladder stile. A path next to a wall on the right

WHILE YOU'RE THERE

Take a look at nearby Edensor, pronounced Ensor. It was built on the instructions of the 6th Duke of Devonshire, who had earlier decided that the gardens of Chatsworth would look much better without the estate houses and duly demolished them. He re-housed the occupants in the purpose built, but very attractive, village of Edensor. The spired 19th-century church has many memorials to the Cavendish family, and there's a marble slab dedicated to Kathleen Kennedy, the sister of President John F Kennedy.

continues above the gritstone crags of Dobb Edge.

Ignore the next stile. Instead bear left on a path down a grassy gully. Emerging into the open parkland once more, head west and cross the road from Park Lodge. Follow the perimeter of the woodland on the other side, round left to the kissing gate. Through this, return on the outward route back to Baslow and the car park.

WHERE TO EAT AND DRINK

The Cafe on the Green in Baslow serves excellent food, including tea, coffee, cakes, and light meals. The Devonshire Arms, in Baslow, serves very good and varied bar meals. There's a cafeteria in Chatsworth House. It is quite expensive, but serves some nice quiches and cakes.

Linacre's Peaceful Retreat from Chesterfield

Three reservoirs secreted between the Chatsworth moors and Chesterfield.

DISTANCE *5 miles (8km)* **MINIMUM TIME** *3hrs*

ASCENT/GRADIENT *820ft (250m)* ▲▲▲ **LEVEL OF DIFFICULTY** +++

PATHS *Generally good paths and farm lanes, field paths can be muddy at times of high rainfall*

LANDSCAPE *Wooded valley and pastured hillsides*

SUGGESTED MAP *OS Explorer OL24 White Peak*

START/FINISH *Grid reference: SK 336727*

DOG FRIENDLINESS *Farmland, dogs should be kept under close control*

PARKING *Linacre Woods car park*

PUBLIC TOILETS *Near car park by Ranger's office*

It is easy to forget, as you look across Linacre and the valley of Holme Brook today, that Chesterfield is only a few miles away. This tranquil combe is sheltered from the west winds by the high Pennine heather moors. Three reservoirs are surrounded by attractive woodland. Linacre means arable land where flax is grown and, as early as the 13th century, linen from that flax was manufactured in the valley. But until the mid-19th century this was no more than an agricultural backwater of north-east Derbyshire.

Good Supply

It was the growth of Chesterfield and the Derbyshire coalfields, and their need for water, that brought the valley to notice. Here was a good supply, well fed by moors to the east. The reservoirs were built between 1855 and 1904 in an attempt to satisfy ever-growing demands. Until 1909, when they built the filter beds, water was pumped direct from the reservoirs to consumers' homes. According to the information sign at Linacre Reservoir the 'water supply was such that the poor used it as soup, the middle class for washing their clothes and the elite for watering their gardens'.

If you have parked on the middle car park, you are standing above the ruins of two great buildings. Not much is known about the older Linacre Hall other than its mention in old charters, but the three-storey mansion of Linacre House was once home to Dr Thomas Linacre (1460–1524), who was president of the Royal College of Surgeons and physician to both Henry VIII and the young Mary, Queen of Scots.

Some steps take you down to the dam of the middle reservoir, and through peaceful Linacre Wood. Although many conifers have been planted for the protection of the reservoirs, about two thirds of the trees are broad-leaved, mainly sycamore, beech, oak and ash. The remaining third are larch, pine and spruce. Hidden in the woods you may discover the remains of some old Q-holes. These were crudely dug pits of about 5ft (1.5m) diameter where timber was once burnt for use in the smelting of lead ore. This was a widespread practice in the 17th century.

Out of Time

Beyond the reservoirs the route climbs out through a wooded clough passing the hillside hamlet of Wigley before descending into the next valley by the ancient track of Bagthorpe Lane. Frith Hall near the valley bottom has a large medieval cruck-framed barn.

The route climbs back out of the valley to Old Brampton. This straggling village is dominated by the broad-spired tower of the 14th-century parish Church of St Peter and St Paul. The oak doors came from the chapel of Derwent Hall before it was submerged beneath Ladybower Reservoir (see Walk 13). Take a closer look at the clock. Can you notice the mistake? It has 63 minutes painted on its face. That gives you a bit more time to stroll down a walled lane to get back to Linacre Wood.

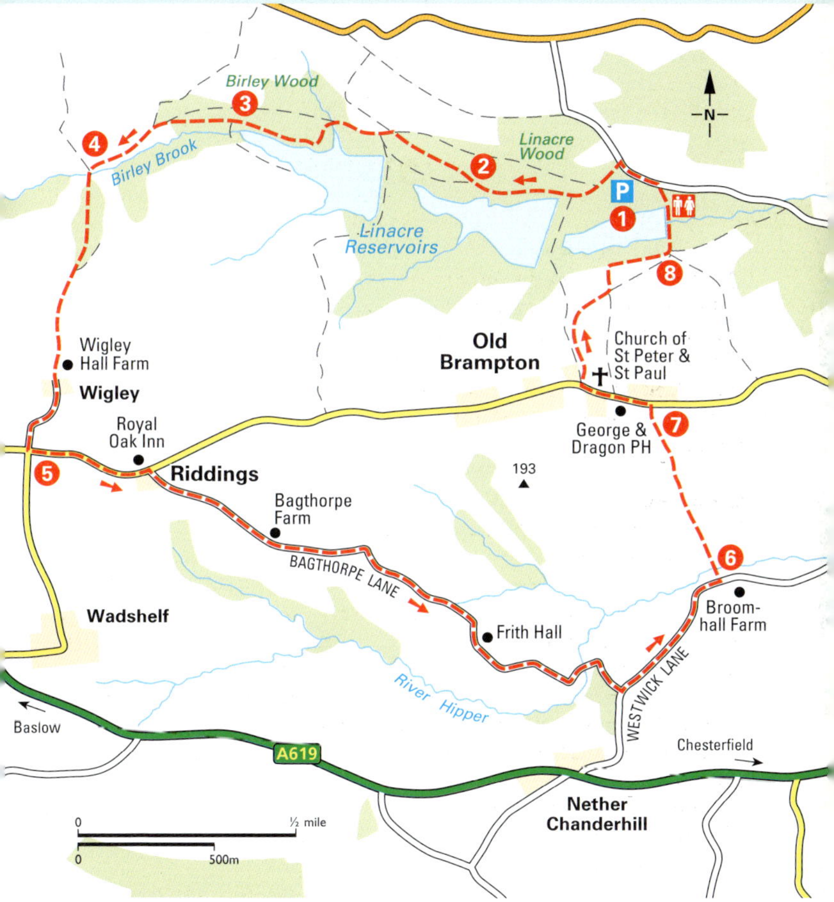

WALK 26 DIRECTIONS

1 From the bottom of the lowest car park go down the steps into the woods. After about 100yds (91m) turn right along a waymarked bridleway heading westwards, high above the lower reservoir. Ignore the path going off to the left, which goes to the dam of the middle reservoir, but continue on the wide bridleway along the north shore of the middle reservoir.

2 Take the right fork on a footpath raking up to the top end of the woods, high above the upper reservoir's dam. The path continues westwards, dipping to one of the reservoir's inlets. Cross over the lower of two bridges and then follow a well-defined concessionary footpath along the lovely shoreline.

3 On reaching the end of the reservoir ignore the left turn over the Birley Brook footbridge, but head west on the waymarked footpath. This soon leaves the woods via a ladder stile and goes straight on through scrub woodland and along the foot of an open slope.

4 Go left over a wooden footbridge and then cross a stone slab over the brook, and go straight on. A muddy path now climbs through more woods before emerging in fields north of Wigley Hall Farm. It passes to the right of the farm to a tarmac lane in the small hamlet of Wigley. Follow the lane to a crossroads.

5 Turn left towards Old Brampton. Just beyond the Royal Oak pub turn right down a tarmac bridleway, Bagthorpe Lane, following it past Bagthorpe Farm. The lane, now unsurfaced, descends into the valley of the River Hipper, passing through the farmyard of Frith Hall, down to the river bridge. A winding surfaced track climbs to Westwick Lane, where you should turn left.

WHERE TO EAT AND DRINK

The George and Dragon, located on the walk opposite the church at Old Brampton, is open all day and extends a warm welcome to walkers.

WHAT TO LOOK FOR

In spring, the woodland floor is covered with bluebells and wild garlic. On the water you'll probably see moorhens and mallards and maybe some of the migrating wildfowl that frequently visit.

6 Just before Broomhall Farm, descend left on another track down to the river, then continue up the other side of the valley into Old Brampton.

7 Turn left along the lane, passing the George and Dragon pub and the church, before turning right by a telephone kiosk. The cart track descends to the top edge of Linacre Wood, then swings to the right.

8 At a junction of paths turn left and descend to the dam. At the far side of the dam turn left on the metalled lane, passing the public conveniences and ranger's office and climb back to the car park.

WHILE YOU'RE THERE

Chesterfield is well worth a visit. It's a historic town dating back to Roman times. The parish church has a curious crooked spire. One of the more credible theories for the leaning is that the Black Death killed off many of the craftsmen of the time, and those left used unseasoned timber that buckled with the weight of the leading.

Through Monsal Dale, the Valley of the Gods

Following the ever-changing River Wye from Ashford-in-the-Water through lovely Monsal Dale.

DISTANCE *5.5 miles (8.8km)* **MINIMUM TIME** *3hrs 30min*

ASCENT/GRADIENT *656ft (200m)* ▲▲▲ **LEVEL OF DIFFICULTY** +++

PATHS *Well-defined paths and tracks throughout, lots of stiles*

LANDSCAPE *Limestone dales and high pasture*

SUGGESTED MAP *OS Explorer OL24 White Peak*

START/FINISH *Grid reference: SK 194696*

DOG FRIENDLINESS *Livestock in Monsal Dale, dogs should be on lead*

PARKING *Ashford-in-the-Water car park*

PUBLIC TOILETS *At car park*

The Wye is a chameleon among rivers. Rising as a peaty stream from Axe Edge, it rushes downhill, only to be confined by the concrete and tarmac of Buxton, a spa town, and the quarries to the east. Beyond Chee Dale it gets renewed vigour and cuts a deep gorge through beds of limestone, finally to calm down again among the gentle fields and hill slopes of Bakewell. The finest stretch of the river valley must be around Monsal Head, and the best approach is that from Ashford-in-the-Water, one of Derbyshire's prettiest villages found just off the busy A6.

Monsal Dale

After passing through Ashford's streets the route climbs to high pastures that give no clue as to the whereabouts of Monsal Dale. But suddenly you reach the last wall and the ground falls away into a deep wooded gorge. John Ruskin was so taken with this beauty that he likened it to the Vale of Tempe: 'you might have seen the Gods there morning and evening – Apollo and the sweet Muses of light – walking in fair procession on the lawns of it and to and fro among the pinnacles of its crags'.

The Midland Railway

It's just a short walk along the rim to reach one of Derbyshire's best-known viewpoints, where the Monsal Viaduct spans the gorge. Built in 1867 as part of the Midland Railway's line to Buxton, the five-arched, stone-built viaduct is nearly 80ft (25m) high. But the building of this railway angered Ruskin. He continued, 'you blasted its rocks away, heaped thousands of tons of shale into its lovely stream. The valley is gone and the Gods with it'.

The line closed in 1968 and the rails were ripped out, leaving only the trackbed and the bridges. Ironically, today's conservationists believe that those are worth saving and have slapped a conservation order on the viaduct. The trackbed is used as a recreational route for walkers and cyclists – the Monsal Trail. The walk continues over the viaduct, giving bird's-eye views of the river and the lawn-like surrounding pastures. It then descends to the river bank, following it westwards beneath the prominent peak of Fin Cop.

The valley curves like a sickle, while the path weaves in and out of thickets, and by wetlands where tall bulrushes and irises grow. After crossing the A6 the route takes you into the mouth of Deep Dale then the shade of Great Shacklow Wood. Just past some pools filled with trout there's an entrance to the Magpie Mine Sough. The tunnel was built in 1873 to drain the Magpie Lead Mines at nearby Sheldon. Magpie was worked intermittently for over 300 years before finally closing in the 1960s. It's believed to be haunted by the ghosts of miners from the neighbouring Redsoil Mine who tragically died underground in a dispute with the Magpie men.

Looking back on the beauty of the day's walk it's hard to believe that the gods haven't returned, or at least given the place a second look.

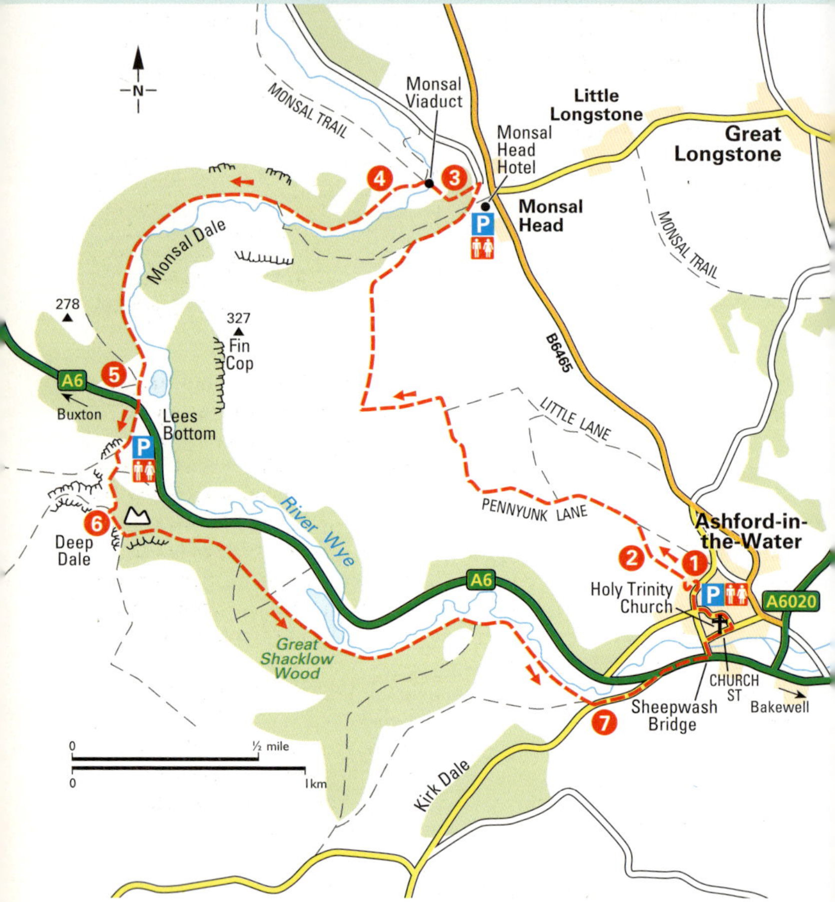

WALK 27 DIRECTIONS

1 From Ashford-in-the-Water car park, walk out to the road and turn right to walk along Vicarage Lane. After 100yds (91m), a footpath on the left doubles back left, then swings sharp right to continue along a ginnel behind a row of houses. Beyond a stile the path enters a field.

2 Head for a stile in the top left corner, then veer slightly right to locate a stile allowing the route to go on to Pennyunk Lane. This

WHAT TO LOOK FOR

Ashford's much-photographed 17th-century Sheepwash Bridge over the River Wye was built on the original site of the ford that gave the village its name. On the far side of the bridge are the enclosures where the sheep were gathered for washing. The square-towered Norman Church of Holy Trinity has an interesting 'black marble' tympanium over the door. The marble is an impure local limestone, which becomes shiny and black when polished.

walled stony track winds among high pastures. At its end go left uphill along a field-edge. At the top it joins another track, heading north (right) towards the rim of Monsal Dale. The path runs along the top edge of the deep wooded dale to reach the car park at Monsal Head.

3 Take the path marked 'Viaduct and Monsal Trail' here – this way you get to walk across the viaduct. On the other side of the viaduct go through a gate on the left. Ignore the path climbing west up the hillside, but descend south-west on a grassy path raking through scrub woods down into the valley. This shouldn't be confused with the steep eroded path plummeting straight down to the foot of the viaduct.

4 Now you walk down the pleasant valley. The right of way is well away from the river at first but most walkers trace the river bank to emerge at Lees Bottom and a roadside stile.

5 Cross the A6 with great care and go through the White Lodge car park on the path the other side, where the route back to Ashford begins. Beyond the gate carry on along the path, ignoring the turning to Toddington. Go over a wall stile and then up to a rocky path, forking left for the path into Great Shacklow Wood, signposted 'Ashford'.

WHERE TO EAT AND DRINK

The Monsal Head Hotel Stables bar serves a wide variety of bar meals. So does the popular Bulls Head in Ashford, which is a Robinsons House and a traditional village pub.

6 The path now climbs steeply through the trees and stony ground to another gate. Ignore the turning right for Sheldon and continue straight ahead, following a fine ledge path along the steep wooded slopes. Eventually the path comes down to the river, past an old mill, before joining a minor road at the bottom of Kirk Dale.

7 Turn left along the road, down to the A6 and turn right towards Ashford. Leave the road to cross Sheepwash Bridge. Turn right along Church Street, then left along Court Lane to the car park.

WHILE YOU'RE THERE

Bakewell, next door to Ashford, is well worth a visit. The spired church of All Saints looks down on this bustling town, which is built round a fine 14th-century bridge over the River Wye. The 13th-century church was refurbished in Victorian times but has many interesting monuments, including one in the Vernon Chapel dedicated to Sir George Vernon, 'King of the Peak'. In the churchyard are two Saxon preaching crosses. The famous Bakewell Pudding Shop is also a popular venue for those who want to taste the real thing.

Overleaf: Monsal Head, Peak District National Park (Walk 27)

WALK 28

Lead Mining and the Transparent Stream

Lathkill Dale contrasts the wastes of a long-past lead-mining industry with the purity of its water.

DISTANCE *5 miles (8km)* **MINIMUM TIME** *3hrs*

ASCENT/GRADIENT *984ft (300m)* ▲▲▲ **LEVEL OF DIFFICULTY** +++

PATHS *Generally well-defined paths. Limestone dale sides can be slippery after rain, lots of stiles*

LANDSCAPE *Partially wooded limestone dales*

SUGGESTED MAP *OS Explorer OL24 White Peak*

START/FINISH *Grid reference: SK 203657*

DOG FRIENDLINESS *Keep dogs on lead*

PARKING *Over Haddon pay car park*

PUBLIC TOILETS *At car park*

Lathkill is, by many degrees, the purest, the most transparent stream that I ever yet saw either at home or abroad...

Charles Cotton, 1676

Today, when you descend the winding lane into this beautiful limestone dale, you are confronted by a seemingly timeless scene of ash trees growing beneath tiered limestone crags, tumbling screes, multi pastel-coloured grasslands swaying in the breeze and that same crystal-clear stream, still full of darting trout.

Invasion of the Lead Miners

Yet it was not always so. In the 18th and 19th centuries lead miners came here and stripped the valley of its trees. They drilled shafts and adits into the white rock, built pump houses, elaborate aqueducts, waterwheels and tramways; and when the old schemes failed to realise profits they came up with new, even bigger ones. Inevitably nobody made any real money, and by 1870 the price of lead had slumped from overseas competition and the pistons stopped.

On this walk you will see the fading remnants of this past, juxtaposed with the natural world that is gradually reclaiming the land. In reality it's Natural England, who are managing the grasslands and woods as part of the Derbyshire Dales National Nature Reserve. Your route starts on a narrow winding lane from Over Haddon to a clapper bridge by Lathkill Lodge. A lush tangle of semi-aquatic plants surround the river and the valley sides are thick with ash and sycamore. In spring you're likely to see nesting moorhens and mallards. In the midst of the trees are some mossy pillars, the remains of an aqueduct built to supply a head of water for the nearby Mandale Mine. The path leaves the woods and the character of the dale changes again. Here sparse ash trees grow out of the limestone screes, where herb Robert adds splashes of pink.

Disappearing River

In the dry periods of summer the river may have disappeared completely beneath its permeable bed of limestone. The sun-dried soils on the southern slopes are too thin to support the humus-loving plants of the valley bottom. Instead, here you'll see the pretty early purple orchid, cowslips with their yellowy primrose-like flowers and clumps of the yellow-flowered rock rose.

After climbing out of Cales Dale the walk traverses the high fields of the White Peak plateau. If you haven't already seen them, look out for Jacob's ladder, a 3ft (1m) tall, increasingly rare plant with clusters of bell-like purple-blue flowers.

By the time you have crossed the little clapper bridge by Lathkill Lodge and climbed back up that winding lane to the car park, you'll have experienced one of Derbyshire's finest dales.

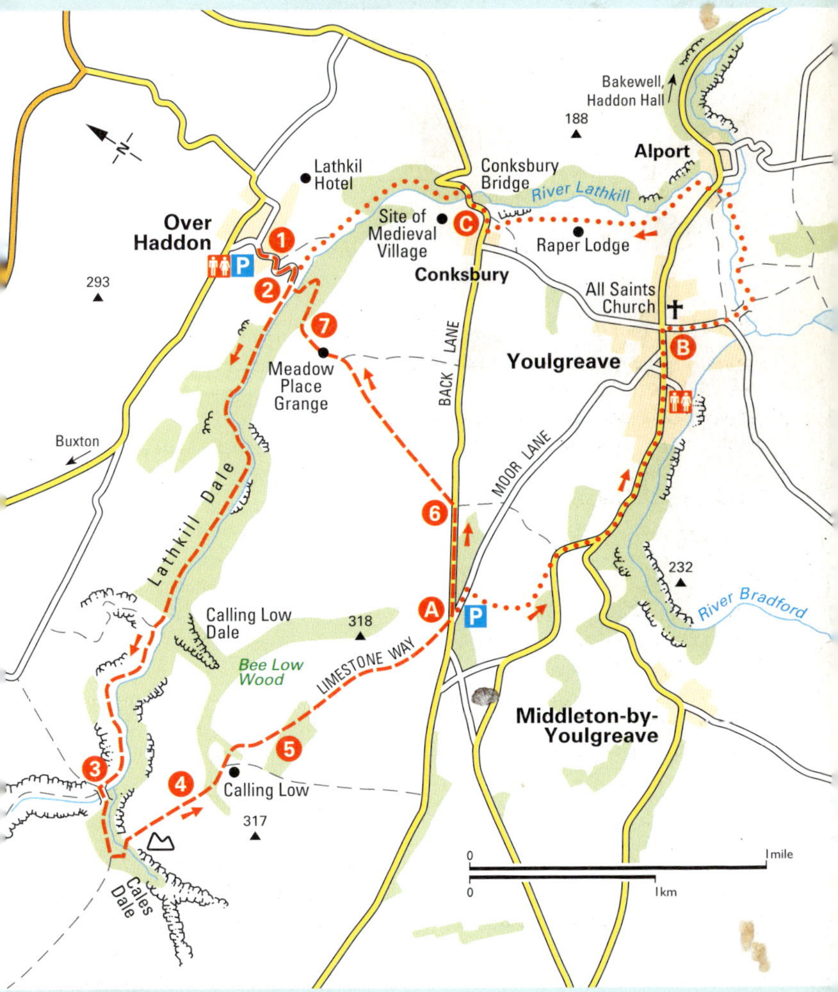

WALK 28 DIRECTIONS

1 Turn right out of the car park, and descend the narrow tarmac lane, which winds down into Lathkill Dale.

2 Just before reaching Lathkill Lodge and the river, turn right along a concessionary track that runs parallel to the north bank. The path passes several caves and a mineshaft as it weaves its way through woodland and thick vegetation. South of Haddon Grove the trees thin to reveal the crags and screes of the upper dale. The path now becomes rougher as it traverses an area of screes.

3 At a junction of routes go over the footbridge and follow a little path sneaking into Cales Dale. Take the left fork down to a stile at the valley bottom. You now join the Limestone Way long distance route on a very steep, stepped path climbing eastwards out of the dale and on to the high pastures of Calling Low.

4 The path heads east of south-east across fields then, just before Calling Low farm, diverts left (waymarked) through several small wooded enclosures. The path swings right beyond the farm, then half left across a cow-pocked field to its top left-hand corner and some woods.

WHAT TO LOOK OUT FOR

Calling Low Grange and Meadow Place Grange, seen en route, were once farmed by monks; the former by the Cistercian order of Roche Abbey in Yorkshire, and the latter by the Augustinian order of Our Lady of Meadows (Leicester). The monks would have tended sheep for the then lucrative wool trade. Today, both farms concentrate on dairy produce.

WHERE TO EAT AND DRINK

The Lathkil Hotel, at the far eastern end of Over Haddon, enjoys one of the best settings of any pub in the Peaks, with breathtaking views across the dale to Youlgreave and the White Peak. Restaurant and bar meals are served daily, lunchtime and evening, and the pub has won several awards for its selection of real ales. Under-14s are not allowed in the main bar.

5 Over steps in the wall the path cuts a corner through the woods before continuing through more fields to a tarmac lane; turn left.

6 After about 500yds (457m), follow a signposted footpath that begins at a stile in a dry-stone wall on the left. This heads north-east across fields to a huge farming complex, Meadow Place Grange. Waymarks show the way across the cobbled courtyard, where the path continues between two stable blocks into another field.

7 After heading north across the field to the brow of Lathkill Dale, turn right through a gate on to a zig-zag track descending to the river. Cross the old clapper bridge to Lathkill Lodge and follow the outward route, a tarmac lane, back to the car park.

WHILE YOU'RE THERE

Nearby Haddon Hall, home of the Dukes of Rutland, is well worth a visit. This 14th-century country house is as impressive as Chatsworth in its own way, with beautifully laid out gardens surrounding a Gothic-style main building. See the fine medieval Banqueting Hall, and the Long Gallery, with its Renaissance panelling. There's a Rex Whistler (1905–1944) painting depicting the 9th Duke and his son.

YOULGREAVE

Lathkill Dale, Bradford Dale and Youlgreave

Youlgreave offers a longer circular walk combining Bradford Dale, which it overlooks, with Lathkill and Cales Dale.

See map and information panel for Walk 28

DISTANCE *8 miles (13km)* **MINIMUM TIME** *5hrs*

ASCENT/GRADIENT *980ft (300m)*▲▲▲ **LEVEL OF DIFFICULTY** +++

WALK 29 DIRECTIONS (Walk 28 option)

Take a little more time in this area and you'll find another beautiful dale and the village of Youlgreave.

Follow Walk 28 to the road beyond Point 5. Instead of turning left follow the right fork, Moor Lane, to the car park. From here a track leads the route south before swinging left down to another road overlooking the pleasantly wooded Bradford Dale.

Follow the road left into Youlgreave, passing the youth hostel, which is an old converted Co-op building, and the Bull's Head Hotel to reach All Saints Church (Point B).

The church has a magnificent Perpendicular tower and a largely Norman nave. Inside is the alabaster tomb of Thomas Cokayne of Harthill Hall, who was killed in a brawl in 1488.

Turn right by the church and follow the road down towards the River Bradford. Where the road bends right, turn left on a track descending behind a house to a footbridge across the river.

After crossing the footbridge turn left and trace the south bank beneath the woods and limestone cliffs of Rheinstor. The route crosses the river by an old packhorse bridge and continues to the road just west of Alport. The village, sited by the confluence of the Bradford and Lathkill rivers, has some lovely 17th- and 18th-century cottages.

Staggered right across the road, the next footpath begins at a gate, the first of many, and continues over fields and parallel to the River Lathkill. After passing beneath the gaunt mansion of Raper Lodge the path meets Conksbury Lane, just west of Conksbury Bridge, (Point B). The site of a medieval village lies on the hillside near Conksbury Farm.

Go over the bridge, then turn left on the path running alongside the Lathkill's east bank. After passing Lathkill Lodge, turn right to climb back up the tarmac lane to the car park at Over Haddon.

WALK 30

Clay Cross Mining and the Five Pits Walk

The industrial landscape around Clay Cross has been transformed by reclamation of old colliery land.

DISTANCE *7 miles (11.3km)* **MINIMUM TIME** *3hrs 30min*

ASCENT/GRADIENT *230ft (70m)* ▲▲▲ **LEVEL OF DIFFICULTY** +++

PATHS *Good surfaced tracks*

LANDSCAPE *Farmland*

SUGGESTED MAP *OS Explorer 269 Chesterfield and Alfreton*

START/FINISH *Grid reference: SK 430624*

DOG FRIENDLINESS *Good, though watch out for bicycle riders*

PARKING *Five Pits Trail car park, Hardstoft road, Pilsley*

PUBLIC TOILETS *None on route*

WALK 30 DIRECTIONS

Look at an old map of Clay Cross and you'll see numerous collieries and a network of railway lines and sidings serving them. Before the decline of the 1970s and 80s, coal played a big part in the lives of north-east Derbyshire folk, and the pits' closures hit them hard. Sadly, in an age when industrial heritage sites are promoted as tourist attractions, not even an old pit wheel seems to have been left to remind us of this proud but dangerous industrial legacy.

Between 1979 and 1989 Derbyshire County Council reclaimed the vast acres of derelict, former colliery land by planting trees and creating fine habitats for wildlife. They have also created the Five Pits Trail, a linear recreational bridleway, with a loop route around Holmewood. Using the trackbeds of the old railways and sidings the route links the pits of Tibshelf and Grassmoor, and then passes through those of Pilsley, Holmewood and Williamthorpe.

To save using two cars, this walk starts at Pilsley, north of Tibshelf, and does the loop around Holmewood before returning to base. The walk begins at the site of Pilsley Station on the old Great Central Railway, which carried coal from the pits to London. The nearby terraced houses were built for the railway's staff.

Across the road from the car park, follow a surfaced track, clearly

WHILE YOU'RE THERE

There are three fascinating buildings in the region. Strangest is the gaunt hilltop castle of Bolsover, which can be seen for miles around. Built in the early 17th century for Charles Cavendish, it replaced a Norman castle built by William Peverel. Sutton Scarsdale Hall, a grand Baroque mansion, is now a shell but was built in 1724 for the 4th Earl of Scarsdale. The six-towered Hardwick Hall, owned by the National Trust, was built in 1590 for Bess of Hardwick. This replaced the house of her birth, the old hall, which lies in ruins in the same grounds.

marked the Five Pits Way, and head northwards with recently planted trees to the right and rolling fields to the left.

On reaching some pines at the edge of the Locko Plantation, the path descends through shady bowers to cross Locko Lane. It continues north, entering Broomridding Wood, which was once used for making charcoal for a neighbouring iron foundry.

On reaching Timber Lane, go through the car park, then turn left across more farm pastures. Take the right fork track, signposted 'Five Pits Trail – Holmewood', which eventually reaches Tibshelf Road. The continuing track is staggered slightly left across the road. The old Holmewood Colliery was sited on the left – it's now an industrial estate. Follow the trail to its junction with A6175 at Holmewood.

Cross, and continue along the obvious, waymarked route opposite. Over the road bridge, then turn sharp left along a waymarked route, passing to the right of a modern industrial estate into recently planted woodland. The track arcs left, and the twisted spire of Chesterfield's church comes into view.

At the second crossroads of tracks, turn left along a wide, firm path heading down towards the Williamthorpe Ponds.

The route doubles back right on a track climbing above the west shores of the ponds, and then by one of the outflow leats. At the next T-junction of tracks, turn left to head south-west. To the right the flattened spoil heaps of the old tip are now covered with the saplings of rowan, sycamore and beech, with colourful broom lining the track.

Take the left fork past the huge sheds of an industrial estate. The track goes under a road bridge, passes to the left of a small pool, then right of Wolfie Pond. You may see the odd mute swan foraging in the rushes, a few mallards and a score of Canada geese competing with the local anglers for a catch.

Just beyond the pool, turn sharply to the left, following the track between North Wingfield and Highfield. Cross the busy A6175 with care and go through the gate on the other side. The track soon bends sharp left, then sharp right to meet the outward route 400yds (366m) north of Timber Lane. Follow the route back to the car park at Pilsley.

WHERE TO EAT AND DRINK

There are no good pubs on the route of this walk, but it's worth a detour at the end of the day to the Winsick Arms in the nearby village of Winsick. Here you'll find they serve a range of good real ales, including Boddingtons and Flowers and excellent traditional English food which includes a highly commendable steak and kidney pie.

WHAT TO LOOK OUT FOR

Williamthorpe Ponds once provided a head of water for the pit engine. They have now been transformed into the centrepiece of an excellent nature reserve. Surrounded by scrub, bulrushes and wetland plants they support an ever-growing number of wildfowl. The facilities include a viewing hide, so it is well worth remembering your binoculars.

WALK 31

Strutting the Ancient Tracks of Beaurepaire

A pleasing ramble around Belper and the surrounding countryside, once a Norman hunting ground.

DISTANCE *5 miles (8km)* **MINIMUM TIME** *3hrs 30min*

ASCENT/GRADIENT *590ft (180m)* ▲▲▲ **LEVEL OF DIFFICULTY** +++

PATHS *Good paths and track, could be muddy after periods of heavy rain, quite a few stiles*

LANDSCAPE *Urban start and finish, but mostly rolling farm pastures*

SUGGESTED MAP *OS Explorer 259 Derby*

START/FINISH *Grid reference: SK 346481*

DOG FRIENDLINESS *Dogs should be kept on lead through farmland*

PARKING *Derwent Valley Visitor Centre, North Mill, Belper*

PUBLIC TOILETS *Nearby Bridge Street*

Before Jedediah Strutt came to Belper, it was just a mere backwater of Derbyshire, and according to Dr Davies, writing in 1811 was 'backward in civility' and considered as the insignificant residence of a few 'uncivilised nailors'. The land around Belper was part of the Norman hunting grounds of Beaurepaire, which meant beautiful retreat. The land was first handed to Henri de Ferrieres and the family ruled here until 1266, when Henry III handed them over to his son the Earl of Leicester, known as Edmund Crouchback.

Strutt's Legacy

Jedediah Strutt had earlier partnered Richard Arkwright in the building of the world's first water-powered cotton mill, sited upriver at Cromford (see Walk 36). The success of that project prompted him to build the South Mill, here at Belper. By 1786 he had built the timber-framed North Mill. Jedediah died in 1797 but his three sons, William, George and Joseph built on his successes. In 30 years there were five mills in the town, though the original North Mill had to be replaced in 1803 after a damaging fire. The Strutts took an active interest in the welfare of their community, providing good housing for their workforce and schooling for the children. As you walk past the North Mill you can see a bridge connecting it with the mill across the road. Note the gun loopholes in it. They were to protect the mills from Luddites, but fortunately the expected trouble never materialised.

Rural Scenes

Most of the walk is rural, and you're soon tramping through woods and across fields. The small lake you see is now a nature reserve, well known for wildfowl. Farm tracks that wouldn't look out of place in a Gainsborough or Constable landscape take you up the hillside to Belper Lane End.

At the top of the hill you reach Longwalls Lane, which was part of the Saxon Portway road. Archaeological finds show that the lane was in use, not only by the Romans, but prehistoric man. In such times the ridges made safer routes than the swampy forests of the valleys, with their dangerous wild animals. The old highway starts unpromisingly as a tarmac lane, but soon becomes a splendid thicket-lined track, with oak trees, wild flowers and wide views up the Derwent Valley. The monument-topped cliff in the distance is Crich Stand (see Walk 42).

Coming down to Blackbrook the route discovers a delightful woodland track above Lumb Brook. Known locally as Depth o' Lumb the wood is coloured by great swathes of bluebells in spring and Himalayan balsam in summer. After descending the slopes of Chevin Mount, the route returns to Belper by the banks of the Derwent, the river that supplied the power for Derbyshire's role in the Industrial Revolution.

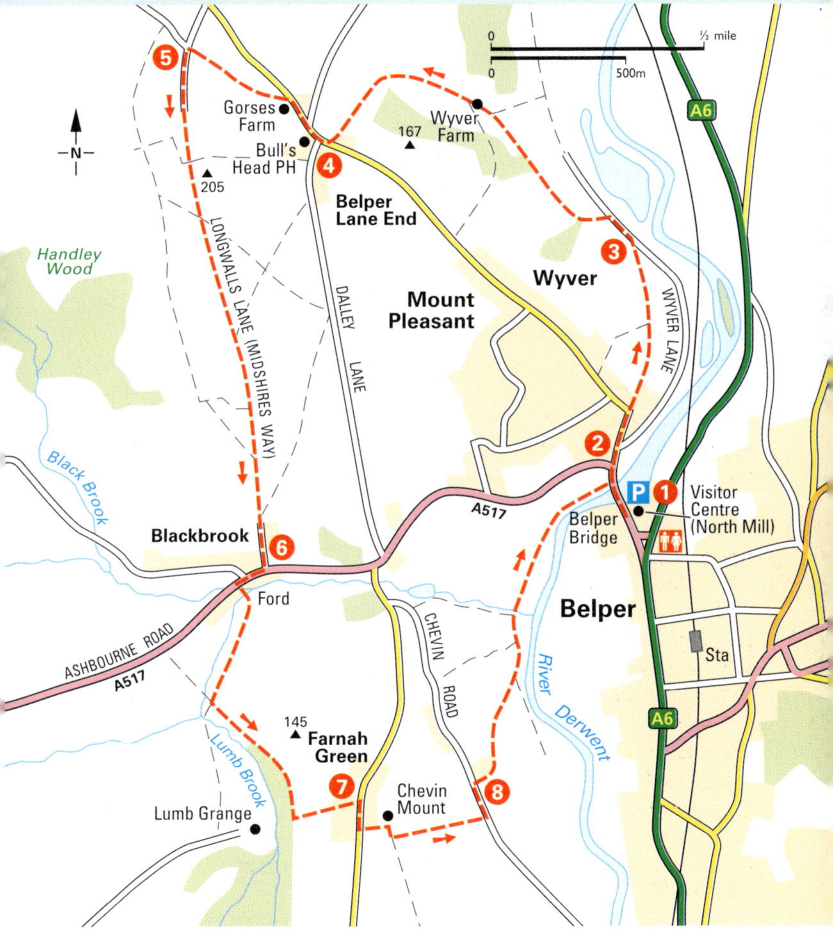

WALK 31 DIRECTIONS

1 From the car park at the visitor centre, turn right on to Belper Bridge over the River Derwent. Cross over the bridge then, when you reach the Talbot Hotel, take the right fork following the signpost 'Belper Lane End and Alderwasley'.

2 Ignore the next right fork, Wyver Lane, but where the road swings sharply left, go straight ahead on a short, unsurfaced lane, called The Scotches. Continue over a stile at the end of the lane for a cross-field path. It finally descends through woodland to reach Wyver Lane opposite a wetlands nature reserve.

3 Turn left along the road for a few paces, then left again on a bridleway track, which arcs left to pass straight through the yard of Wyver Farm before continuing to the road at Belper Lane End.

4 Turn right along the road, passing the Bull's Head pub and then take the left fork to Gorses Farm. Here a farm track climbs past some chicken sheds before reaching a T-junction of country lanes.

WHILE YOU'RE THERE

Why not learn more about the town and its fascinating history. There are two short, self-guided walks around Belper. Leaflets are available at the visitor centre.

5 Turn left along Longwalls Lane, which soon degenerates into a stony track. Continue to follow the track downhill and keep straight ahead along a less well-defined track. In time this becomes a walled path before returning to a proper lane again beyond a large house. The lane then meets Ashbourne Road at Blackbrook.

6 Turn right along the road for about 200yds (183m), then turn left over a footbridge by a ford. Follow the lane for 600yds (549m) to a footpath on the left, highlighted by Midshires Way waymarkers. Go through the squeeze stile and follow the well-defined field path climbing to the south-east. The path enters an area of delightful woodland through Lumb Grange, then turns left at a stile in a wall, aiming for some houses at the far end of a field. Take the right-hand of two parallel tracks, past the houses to reach the road at Farnah Green.

WHAT TO LOOK FOR

Visit the Derwent Valley Visitor Centre at North Mill. It has exhibitions illustrating the development of the region during the Industrial Revolution. You'll see Hargreave's revolutionary Spinning Jenny, Arkwright's Water Frame and Crompton's Mule. In 2001 the Derwent Valley Mills area was designated a World Heritage Site by UNESCO for its industrial heritage.

7 Turn right along the road to walk through the village. After 150yds (137m) follow the Midshires Way along an unsurfaced lane by Chevin Mount. Just beyond the sharp right-hand bend in the lane turn left along a footpath. This descends directly through sloping fields eastwards to Chevin Road.

8 The continuing path is staggered 200yds (183m) to the north and follows a short driveway to the stile at the end. Beyond this go left on a clear footpath across fields and down to the River Derwent. Follow the various riverside paths and tracks back to Belper Bridge and the outward route.

WHERE TO EAT AND DRINK

En route you can get bar snacks in the Bull's Head at Belper Lane End. Belper has several good pubs, including the George and the Lion Hotel on Bridge Street, also there are many cafés and restaurants to choose from.

Pilsbury Castle and the Upper Dove Valley

The upper valley of the Dove has quiet villages and historic remains.

DISTANCE 7.5 miles (12.1km) **MINIMUM TIME** 4hrs
ASCENT/GRADIENT 804ft (245m) ▲▲▲ **LEVEL OF DIFFICULTY** +++
PATHS Field paths and lanes, some steep climbs, lots of stiles
LANDSCAPE Pastures, limestone valley
SUGGESTED MAP OS Explorer OL24 White Peak
START/FINISH Grid reference: SK 127603
DOG FRIENDLINESS Keep dogs on lead
PARKING Parson's Field, Hartington, pay car park
PUBLIC TOILETS Near car park

Hartington, lying in the mid regions of the Dove Valley, is a prosperous village with 18th-century houses and hotels built in local limestone and lined around spacious greens. Its history can be traced back to the Normans, when it was recorded as Hartedun, the centre for the De Ferrier's estate. Hartington Hall, now the youth hostel, was first built in 1350 but was substantially rebuilt in 1611. Bonnie Prince Charlie is reputed to have stopped here in 1745 on his march into Derby, where 5,000 Highland troops were amassing to fight for the Jacobite cause. He didn't know that the Duke of Devonshire had amassed 30,000 loyalists. The Prince would retreat to Scotland, where he would be cruelly dealt with at Culloden.

As you leave the village the lane climbs past the Church of St Giles, which has a battlemented Perpendicular tower. It continues up the high valley sides of the Dove, then on through emerald high fields and valley.

Pilsbury Castle

Pilsbury Castle hides from the viewer until the very last moment, but then a grassy ramp swoops down to it from the hillsides. Only the earthworks are now visible, but you can imagine its supreme impregnable position on the limestone knoll that juts out into the valley. You can see the motte, a man-made mound built to accommodate the wooden keep, and the bailey, a raised embankment that would have had a wooden stockade round it.

The castle's exact history is disputed. It was probably built around 1100 by the Normans, on the site of an Iron Age fort. It may have been a stronghold used earlier by William I to suppress a local rebellion in his 'Wasting of the North' campaign. Being in the middle of the De Ferrier estate it was probably their administrative centre. In the 1200s this function would have been moved to Hartington.

Views up-valley are fascinating, with the conical limestone peaks of Parkhouse and Chrome hills in the distance. Now the route descends into Dovedale for the first time, crossing the river into Staffordshire. The lane climbs to a high lane running the length of the dale's east rim. Note the change in the rock – it's now the darker gritstone. The crags of Sheen Hill have been blocking the view east, but once past them you can see for miles, across the Manifold Valley to the Roaches and Hen Cloud. A field path takes the route on its finale, descending along a line of crags with lofty views.

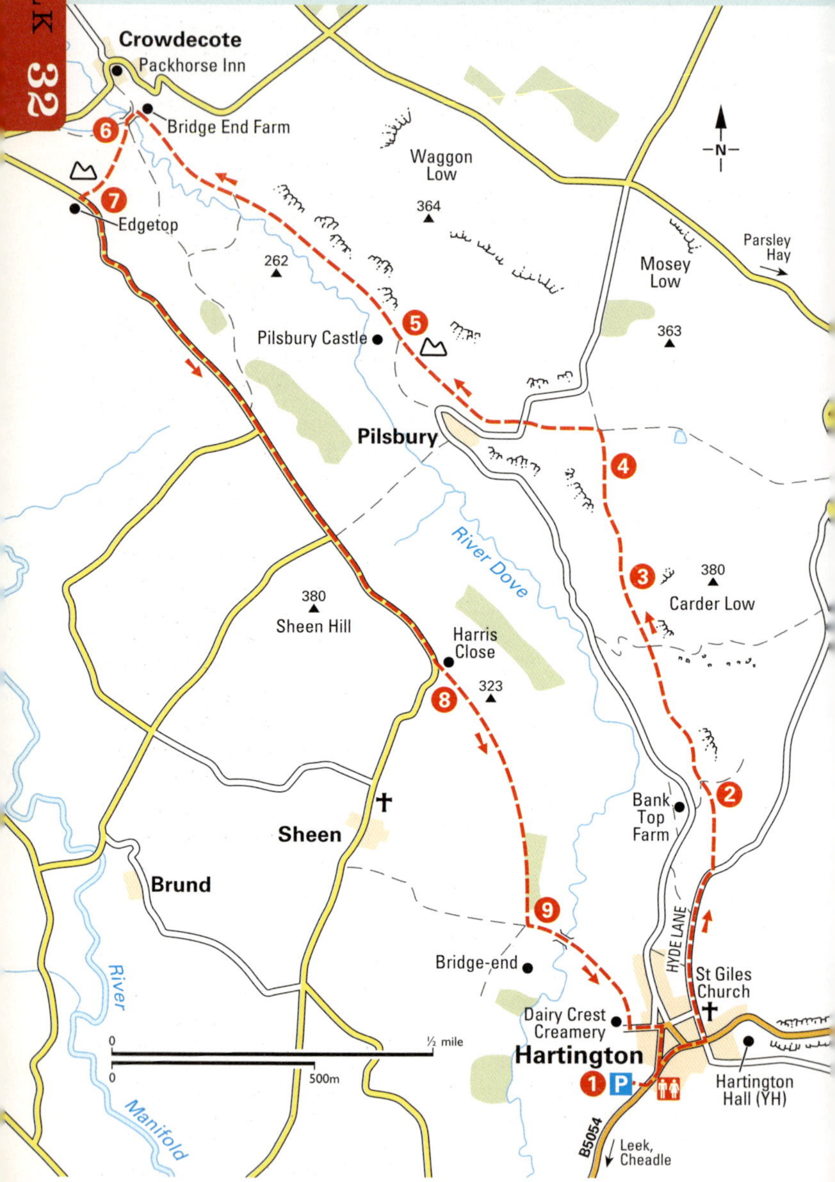

WALK 32 DIRECTIONS

1 Turn left out of the car park and follow the road through the centre of the village. Turn left, uphill by the church on Hyde Lane and then take the third path on the left. This descends northwards across fields. Just below a farmhouse, the path swings left to follow a dry-stone wall on the left.

WHAT TO LOOK OUT FOR

In Hartington the Dairy Crest Creamery is one of the few places licensed to make Stilton. There's a visitor centre where you can sample and buy the cheeses. Look too for Hartington Hall, now a youth hostel.

2 The path cuts across the stony drive coming up the hill from Bank Top Farm. Waymarking posts highlight the continuing route along the high valley sides.

3 West of Carder Low (grid ref 126627) the path goes through a gateway by an intersection of walls and becomes indistinct. Here, climb half right to another gateway, then head for a group of trees. Beyond these another footpath signpost shows the way uphill to a step stile in a ridge wall, where you look down into a small valley.

4 Descend into the valley and turn left to reach a high lane by a stone barn. A stile across the road allows you on to the continuing path, rounding the high slopes above Pilsbury. The footpath rakes left down the hill slopes to a farm track and wall alongside the ancient earthworks of Pilsbury Castle. A gate in the stone wall allows further inspection.

5 Turn right and continue down a grassy track, which eventually degenerates into a field path heading up the valley towards Crowdecote.

6 Just past Bridge End Farm turn left to cross the Dove by a little footbridge. Follow the path directly uphill across a field.

7 Beyond the wall stile the path veers right, through scrub, to reach the Longnore road near Edgetop. Turn left along the high lane to Harris Close Farm.

8 A stile on the nearside of an outbuilding at Harris Close starts the path back to Hartington. In all but one field there's a wall on the right for guidance. After going through a wood, the path descends through scrub into the valley. It joins a farm track southwards towards Bridge-end farm.

WHERE TO EAT AND DRINK

Very good meals are served at the Charles Cotton Hotel at Hartington (free house). They're equally good at the Packhorse Inn at Crowdecote (free house), just 200yds (183m) off route.

9 At the signpost 'Hartington' turn left through a gate and then continue across a field. Spy a footbridge, hidden by trees, which allows you to cross the Dove. The intermittent path gradually swings right (south-east) across fields. The path aims for the woods to the left of the dairy and enters them via a gate. At the other side go through a field beside a dairy and turn left along the lane to return to Hartington.

WHILE YOU'RE THERE

You could visit Arbor Low, 3 miles (5km) north-east near Parsley Hay (English Heritage). This stone circle and henge was constructed between 3000 and 2000 BC, around the same time as Stonehenge. The main circle is over 820ft (250m) in circumference. None of the 60 or so stones are erect but the remote setting beneath the even older tumulus of Gib Hill gives the place a dramatic aura. There's a small charge to see the monument.

Wolfscote Dale and a Railway Trail

Wolfscote Dale and Biggin Dale wind through the heart of the upland limestone country.

DISTANCE *7.5 miles (12.1km)* **MINIMUM TIME** *5hrs*

ASCENT/GRADIENT *557ft (170m)* ▲▲▲ **LEVEL OF DIFFICULTY** +++

PATHS *Generally well-defined paths, limestone dale sides can be slippery after rain; several stiles*

LANDSCAPE *Partially wooded limestone dales and high pasture*

SUGGESTED MAP *OS Explorer OL24 White Peak*

START/FINISH *Grid reference: SK 156549*

DOG FRIENDLINESS *Can run free on trail; on lead in nature reserve*

PARKING *Tissington Trail pay car park near Alsop en le Dale*

PUBLIC TOILETS *None on route*

From its source, on Axe Edge, to Hartington the River Dove is little more than a stream, flowing almost apologetically past the dragon's back at Chrome Hill, and in an attractive but shallow valley south of Crowdecote. But once through the woodlands of Beresford Dale it gets more confident and cuts a deep limestone canyon with cliffs and tors almost equal to those of the more celebrated Dovedale. This canyon is Wolfscote Dale, and it's wilder and more unspoiled than Dovedale, with narrower, less populated paths, and less woodland to hide the crags. Weirs have been constructed to create calm pools that attract trout and grayling to linger.

Compleat Angler

The river here was a great joy to Charles Cotton, a 17th-century poet born in nearby Beresford Hall. Cotton, an enthusiastic young angler, introduced his great friend, Izaak Walton, to the area and taught him the art of fly-fishing. Together they built a fishing temple in the nearby woods of Beresford Dale (in private grounds). They wrote *The Compleat Angler*, a classic collection of fishing stories, published in 1651. Unfortunately Cotton's precarious financial position forced him to sell the hall in 1681, and it now lies in a ruinous state.

Wolfscote Dale

The path up Wolfscote Dale begins at Lode Mill, which still has its waterwheel intact. The river, verged by lush vegetation, has cut a deep and twisting valley through the limestone. The slopes are thickly wooded with ash, sycamore and alder. Further north this woodland thins out to reveal more of the crags, and a ravine opens out to the right of Coldeaton Bridge. The dale, like so many in Derbyshire, is rich in wildlife. Dipper, pied wagtails and grey wagtails often forage along the limestone banks, and if you're quick enough you may see the blue flash of a kingfisher diving for a fish. The dale divides again beneath the magnificent Peaseland Rocks. It's a shame to leave the Dove but Biggin Dale is a pleasing contrast. For most

Left: St Giles parish church, Hartington (Walk 32)

of the year it's a dry valley, but in winter the rocky path may be jostling for room with a newly surfaced stream. It's a narrow dale with limestone screes and scrub gorse. What looks like a natural cave on the right is in fact the entrance to an old lead mine. Through a gate you enter a National Nature Reserve, known for its many species of limestone-loving plants and its butterflies. At the top of the dale you come to Biggin, a straggling village, from where the return route is an easy-paced one, using the Tissington Trail, which ambles over the high plains of Alport Moor.

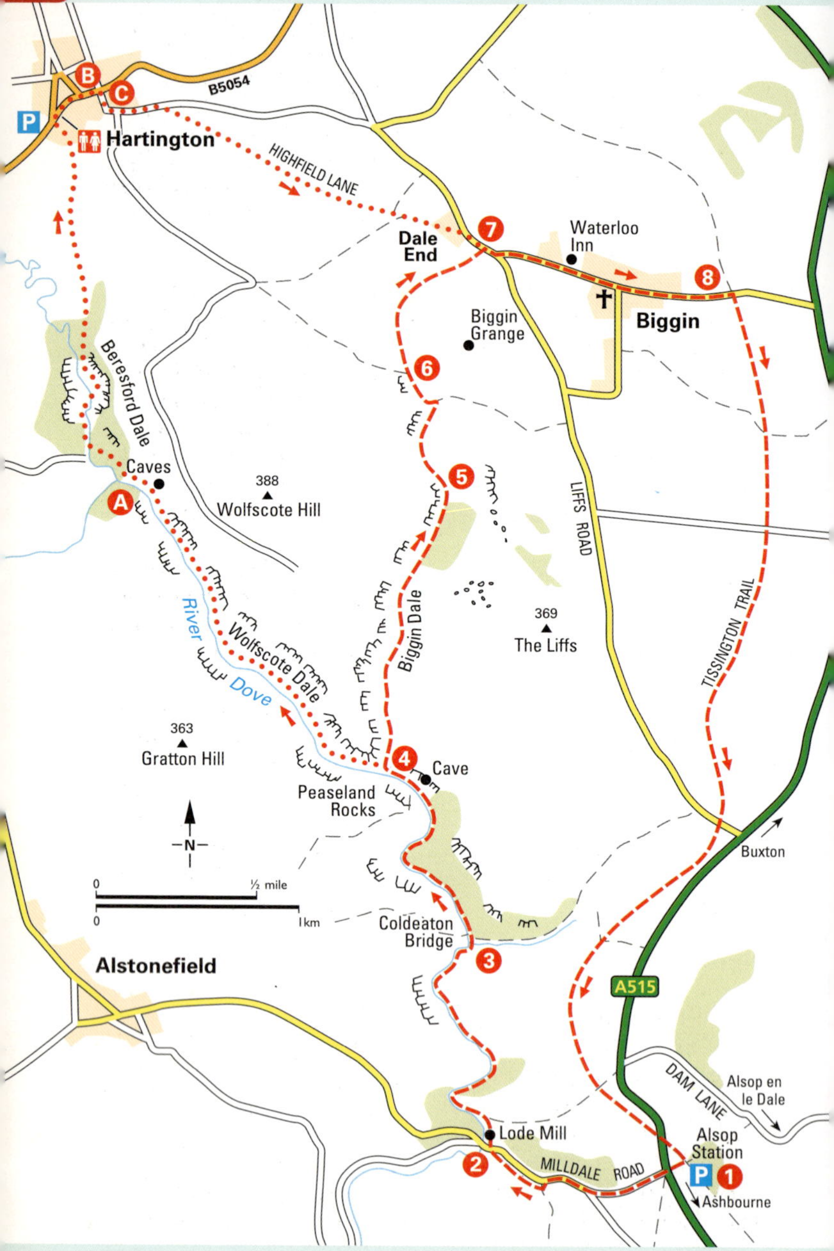

WALK 33 DIRECTIONS

1 From the car park at the former Alsop Station, cross the busy A515 and follow the Milldale Road immediately opposite. After a junction you are offered a parallel footpath on the left, keeping you safe from the traffic.

2 On reaching the bottom of the dale by Lode Mill, turn right along the footpath, tracing the river's east bank through a winding, partially wooded valley.

3 Ignore the footpath on the right at Coldeaton Bridge, but instead stay with Wolfscote Dale beneath thickly wooded slopes on the right. Beyond a stile the woods cease and the dale becomes bare and rock-fringed, with a cave on the right and the bold pinnacles of Peaseland Rocks ahead. Here the valley sides open out into the dry valley of Biggin Dale, where this route goes next.

4 The signposted path into Biggin Dale begins beyond a gate in a cross-wall and follows that wall. It continues through scrub woodland and beneath limestone screes. Beyond a gate you enter a nature reserve.

5 There is another gate at the far end of the nature reserve. Beyond the gate, the dale curves left, then right, before dividing again beneath the hill pastures of Biggin Grange. Divert left here, through a gate to follow the footpath, signposted to Hartington. On the other side of the wall there is a concrete dewpond.

WHERE TO EAT AND DRINK

The Waterloo Inn at Biggin is an ideal place for a refreshment break before heading back on the trail. If you're looking for a delicious bar meal at the end of the day, drive a couple of miles south along the A515 to try the Bluebell Inn at Tissington Gate.

WHILE YOU'RE THERE

Why not have a look around Fenny Bentley, an attractive village 3 miles (4.8km) north of Ashbourne. Inside St Edmund's Church are the shrouded effigies to Sir Thomas Beresford, his wife and twenty-one children, who lived in nearby Bentley Hall.

6 After 200yds (183m) there's another junction of paths. Ignore the one signposted to Hartington and keep walking ahead, following the path to Biggin. It stays with the valley round to the right, passing a small sewage works (left) before climbing out of the dale to reach the road at Dale End.

7 Turn right along the road for a few paces then left, following a road past the Waterloo Inn and through Biggin village.

8 On the far side of the former railway bridge towards the top of the hill join the Tissington Trail bridleway. Follow this old trackbed southwards, across the pastures of Biggin and Alport moors, for 2 miles (3.2km) until you reach the car park.

WHAT TO LOOK OUT FOR

In Biggin Dale, besides the rampantly prickly gorse bushes, you should see many limestone loving plants including the purple-flowered meadow cranesbill, patches of delicate harebells, early purple orchids with their dark-spotted stems and leaves and orangy-yellow cowslips.

Beresford Dale

Staying with Wolfscote Dale has its dividends as you emerge in a spectacular section of dales scenery on this longer walk.

See map and information panel for Walk 33

WALK 34

DISTANCE *9.25 miles (15km)* **MINIMUM TIME** *6hrs*

ASCENT/GRADIENT *656ft (200m)* ▲▲▲ **LEVEL OF DIFFICULTY** +++

WALK 34 DIRECTIONS (Walk 33 option)

This is a slightly longer version of Walk 33, in which Biggin Dale is substituted by what some will consider to be the most spectacular part of Wolfscote Dale, its northernmost reaches. It also steps out of Derbyshire for a little while into its neighbouring county, Staffordshire

Follow Walk 33 to the opening of Biggin Dale (Point 4) but this time stay with Wolfscote Dale. By now most of the dale's trees have been replaced by bare grassy slopes interspersed with flowing screes and limestone crags.

After twisting right the valley deepens between Wolfscote and Gratton hills and the river flows over a series of weirs. Soon the valley narrows again, and you see a large cave to the right, Frank i' the Rocks (Point A). Evidence has been found here of both Roman and Anglo Saxon burials.

Ignore a footbridge and continue across a wide riverside field, then cross a wooden footbridge to the west bank of the River Dove. You've just crossed into Staffordshire and Beresford Dale. The path soon realises this, and after a few hundred yards of tucking under the alder woodland it recrosses to the Derbyshire side via another footbridge.

Go over the stile and out of the woods to cross fields with a small limestone hill on the right, and the Dove meandering on the left in its now shallow valley. Head north, keeping to the low, left shoulder of the hill, before crossing a green lane and coming into Hartington.

Turn right beyond the public toilet block, passing through the centre of the village (Point B), and right again by the war memorial. The lane climbs past the 17th-century Hartington Hall (Point C), now a youth hostel. At the end of a row of trees, on the right, go right along a stony walled track, Highfield Lane, signposted 'Biggin'. This climbs south-east across pastureland, before descending to the road at the head of Biggin Dale (Point 7), where it meets Walk 33 and follows it through Biggin village, before continuing along the easy going Tissington Trail back to the car park.

WALK 35

Walking on the Roystone Grange Trail

The National Park's well-planned history trail at Roystone Grange gives a good introduction to walking in the Peak.

DISTANCE *4 miles (6.4km)* **MINIMUM TIME** *2hrs*
ASCENT/GRADIENT *360ft (110m)* ▲▲▲ **LEVEL OF DIFFICULTY** +++
PATHS *Good paths and tracks, fields can be muddy*
LANDSCAPE *Farmland*
SUGGESTED MAP *OS Explorer OL24 White Peak*
START/FINISH *Grid reference: SK 194582*
DOG FRIENDLINESS *Dogs on lead in farmland around livestock*
PARKING *Minninglow car park, near Pikehall*
PUBLIC TOILETS *None on route*

WALK 35 DIRECTIONS

Every hill and valley has a story to tell. At first glance Roystone Grange looks nothing out of the ordinary – just a typical White Peak valley of the Peak District National Park. There is a rather strange-looking group of trees on a hill to the east, but not much else of note. However, archaeologists from Sheffield University carried out diggings over several years and unearthed evidence of the existence of Roman farms and prehistoric camps, and a medieval grange run by Cistercian monks.

The National Park Authority subsequently developed and waymarked the Roystone Grange Trail, which takes you back 6,000 years into history.

From the back of the car park follow the old Cromford and High Peak Railway trackbed eastwards across lofty fields. The track swings south after passing over the first of two huge stone embankments. The railway track goes through a cutting where cowslips and orchids grow, then past an old stone quarry with a rusting crane tucked in the shade of the rockface. Back on to another railway embankment above Minninglow Grange Farm, you'll soon notice a complex of Victorian brick kilns. High-firing silica sands found near the farm were made into bricks here, for use as liners for the steel furnaces of Sheffield.

On reaching the brick kilns, leave the railway trackbed behind and turn left along a track known as Gallowlow Lane. This follows the original boundary of the medieval grange estate and is assumed to have been of medieval, or even of Roman origin.

To the left is Minninglow Hill. The crown of gaunt beech trees hides an ancient barrow, Minning Low. This was excavated in 1851 revealing a very large megalithic chamber and several imperfect cists (stone coffins). One of these, however, was intact and with its capstone in place.

WHILE YOU'RE THERE

You could visit nearby Winster, three miles to the east of Pikehall. It's an old lead-mining village with character in plenty, and most of its housing dating back to the 18th century. Centre stage in Winster however is the 16th-century Old Market Hall, now used as a National Trust information centre. The ground floor used to be open, with pointed stone arches, but they've since been bricked up. The upper floors are of brick. The Trust's purchase of the Hall in 1906 was their first acquisition in the Peak District. The village is also well known for its morris dancers and its annual Shrove Tuesday Pancake Race.

After about 0.25 mile (400m) climb the stile in the right-hand wall, and follow the path under the old railway tunnel. Take the right of two gates in the next crosswall, and then continue down a grassy hollow. A wall comes in from the left and the path runs alongside it. While you are here, look southwards and you should see a Bronze Age barrow on the next hilltop. Mysteriously, several skulls were excavated here without the rest of their skeletons. The dig also revealed two Roman dress pins.

WHERE TO EAT AND DRINK

This is a surprisingly remote area and there's nowhere on the route, but try the Miners Standard just outside Winster to the east, or head north to the George Hotel in Youlgreave.

Go over a stile in the wall, then continue along its left side. Beyond the next crosswall, bear slightly to the left across a field, aiming for the top left-hand corner and in the direction of a building that looks like an old chapel. A stile here gives access to a farm track from Roystone Grange. Turn left here for a short way, before going through the waymarked gate towards the 'chapel'. The building is in fact a pump house whose engine used to send pressurised air to power the pneumatic drills used in the quarries that you saw earlier.

The original Roystone Grange farm, then known as Revestones, was sited between the pump house and the woods behind. In the 14th century the farm was given, by Adam of Herthill, to the Cistercian abbey of Garendon in Leicestershire. Monks and local 'lay brothers' would have worked the sheep farm and sold most of the wool abroad, but hard times would follow after bad winters and the Black Death.

WHAT TO LOOK OUT FOR

You could make a detour along the concessionary route from Roystone Grange to Ballidon. From this track junction 300yds (274m) south of Roystone Grange farm you should be able to pick out the remains of a Roman field system of banks and terraces.

Follow the metalled farm track north, past the modern farm to the disused dairy. The excavations here in 1978–9 unearthed the foundations of an old Roman manor, which stood on the boulder-strewn terrace beyond. The 2nd-century building would have had rubble-built walls and a thatched roof supported by aisle posts.

Turn left along Minninglow Lane which takes you out on to the road proper, leading northwards back to the car park.

Cromford and the Black Rocks

Walk through the Industrial Revolution in a valley where history was made.

DISTANCE *5 miles (8km)* **MINIMUM TIME** *3hrs*

ASCENT/GRADIENT *720ft (220m)* ▲▲▲ **LEVEL OF DIFFICULTY** +++

PATHS *Well-graded – canal tow paths, lanes, forest paths and a railway trackbed, quite a few stiles*

LANDSCAPE *Town streets and wooded hillsides*

SUGGESTED MAP *OS Explorer OL24 White Peak*

START/FINISH *Grid reference: SK 300571*

DOG FRIENDLINESS *Dogs on lead over farmland, can run free on long stretches of enclosed railway trackbed*

PARKING *Cromford Wharf pay car park*

PUBLIC TOILETS *At car park*

For many centuries Cromford, 'the ford by the bend in the river', was no more than a sleepy backwater. Lead mining brought the village brief prosperity, but by the 18th century even that was in decline. Everything changed in 1771 when Sir Richard Arkwright decided to build the world's first water-powered cotton-spinning mill here. Within 20 years he had built two more, and had constructed a whole new town around them. Cromford was awake to the Industrial Revolution and would be connected to the rest of Britain by a network of roads, railways and canals.

As you walk through the cobbled courtyard of the Arkwright Mill, now being restored by the Arkwright Society, you are transported back into that austere world of the 18th century, back to the times when mother, father and children all worked at the mills.

Most of the town actually lies on the other side of the traffic-laden A6, including the mill pond which was built by Arkwright to impound the waters of Bonsall Brook, and the beautifully restored mill workers' cottages of North Street.

The Black Rocks

The Black Rocks overlook the town from the south. The walk makes a beeline for them through little ginnels, past some almshouses and through pine woods. You'll see climbers grappling with the 80ft (24m) gritstone crags, but there's a good path all the way to the top. Here you can look across the Derwent Valley to the gaunt skeleton of Riber Castle, to the beacon on top of Crich Stand and down the Derwent Gorge to Matlock.

The Cromford and High Peak Railway

The next stage of the journey takes you on to the High Peak Trail, which uses the former trackbed of the Cromford and High Peak Railway. Engineered by Josias Jessop and constructed in the 1830s, the railway was built as an extension of the canal system and, as such, the stations were called wharfs.

In the early years horses pulled the wagons on the level stretches, while steam-winding engines worked the inclines. By the mid-1800s steam engines worked the whole line, which connected with the newly extended Midland Railway. The railway was closed by Dr Beeching in 1967.

The Canal

After abandoning the High Peak Trail pleasant forest paths lead you down into the valley at High Peak Junction, where the old railway met the Cromford Canal. The 33-mile (53km) canal was built in 1793, a year after Arkwright's death, to link up with the Erewash, thus completing a navigable waterway to the River Trent at Trent Lock. Today, there's an information centre here, a fascinating place to muse before that final sojourn along the tow path to Cromford.

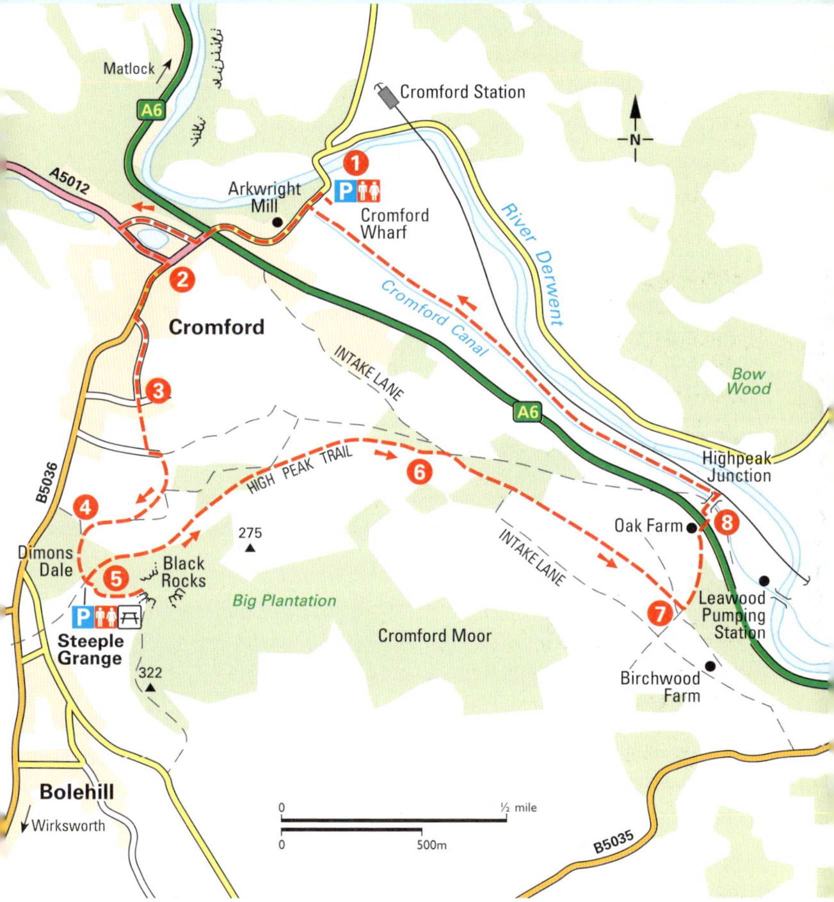

WALK 36 DIRECTIONS

1 Turn left out of the car park on to Mill Road. Cross the A6 to the Market Place. Turn right down Scarthin, passing the Boat Inn and the old millpond before doubling back left along Water Lane to Cromford Hill.

2 Turn right, past the shops and Bell Inn, then turn left up

Bedehouse Lane, which turns into a narrow tarmac ginnel and heads uphill past some almshouses (otherwise known as bedehouses).

3 At the top of the lane by a street of 1970s housing, a signpost for Black Rocks points uphill. The footpath continues its climb southwards to meet a lane. Turn left along the winding lane, which soon divides. Take the right fork, a surfaced track leading to a stone-built house with woods behind. On reaching the house, turn right through a gate, and then follow the top field-edge.

4 After climbing some steps, ascend left through the woods of Dimons Dale up to the Black Rocks car park and picnic site. The track you've reached is on the former trackbed of the Cromford and High Peak Railway. Immediately opposite is the there-and-back waymarked detour leading to the rocks.

5 Returning to the car park, turn right along the High Peak Trail, which traverses the hillside high above Cromford.

6 After 0.75 mile (1.2km) take a path on the right off the incline for Intake Lane. At the lane, turn right and follow it to a sharp right-hand bend. Here, go straight on, following a path heading south-east along the top edge of some woodland. (Please note that neither the path nor the wood is shown on the current OS Explorer OL24 White Peak.)

7 On nearing Birchwood Farm, watch out for two paths coming up from the left. Take the second smaller one descending more directly downhill in a sunken channel. At the bottom of the woods the path swings left across a field, coming out to the A6 road by Oak Farm.

8 Cross the road and follow the little ginnel opposite, over the Cromford Canal by the Highpeak Junction information centre. Turn left before the Matlock Railway and along the canal tow path. Follow this back to the car park at Cromford Wharf.

WHAT TO LOOK OUT FOR

Besides the Arkwright Mill, which is a 'must see', take some time to visit the exhibits in old railway workshops at Highpeak Junction and the Leawood Pumping Station, which pumped water from the River Derwent to the Cromford Canal. The restored Leawood works has a working Cornish-type beam engine.

WHERE TO EAT AND DRINK

Arkwright Mill has a café for coffee, cake and light snacks. The excellent Boat Inn free house on Scarthin at Cromford serves bar meals at lunchtimes and evenings and has a beer garden.

WHILE YOU'RE THERE

If you have time, visit Wirksworth, a former lead-mining town on the hillsides above Cromford. Until a restoration project of the 1980s Wirksworth had become a dusty, derelict place that nobody wanted to visit. Take a look at the National Stone Centre on Portway Lane. Here you can have a go at gem panning and join guided walks. The Wirksworth Heritage Centre, which is housed in a former silk and velvet mill at Crown Yard, gives a fascinating insight into the town's history.

Scaling the Heights of Abraham

A steady climb raises you above the hurly-burly of Matlock Bath to a more familiar Peakland landscape.

DISTANCE *8 miles (12.9km)* **MINIMUM TIME** *4hrs 30min*

ASCENT/GRADIENT *1,200ft (365m)* ▲▲▲ **LEVEL OF DIFFICULTY** +++

PATHS *Narrow woodland paths, field paths and unsurfaced lanes, lots of stiles*

LANDSCAPE *Fields and wooded hillsides*

SUGGESTED MAP *OS Explorer OL24 White Peak*

START/FINISH *Grid reference: SK 297595*

DOG FRIENDLINESS *Dogs on lead over farmland*

PARKING *Pay car park at Artists Corner*

PUBLIC TOILETS *At car park*

Between Matlock and Cromford the River Derwent forges its way through a spectacular, thickly wooded limestone gorge. At Matlock Bath it jostles for space with the bustling A6 highway, the railway to Derby and a string of three-storey houses, shops and amusement parlours, built by the Victorians, who flocked here to take in the healing spa waters. On the hillside to the east lies the gaunt castle of Riber, while Alpine-type cable cars glide up the Heights of Abraham, above cliff tops to the west.

The Heights in Quebec

The original Heights of Abraham, which the hillside must have resembled, rise above Quebec and the St Lawrence River in Canada. There, in 1759, British troops under General Wolfe fought a victorious battle with the French under General Montcalm. Both generals were killed and the encounter earned Wolfe, and Quebec, an unenviable place in English place-name folklore, to be joined later by Waterloo and later still, Spion Kop.

Matlock Bath

Matlock Bath doesn't have time to catch its breath: it's Derbyshire's mini-Blackpool. Yet there are peaceful corners, and this fine walk seeks them out. It offers fine views across the Matlock Gorge. Spurning the cable car, it climbs through the woods and out on to the hillside above the town. The Victoria Prospect Tower peeps over the trees. Built by unemployed miners a century ago it's now part of the Heights of Abraham complex.

Above the complex, a little path leads you through delectable woodland. In spring it's heavy with the scent of wild garlic and coloured by a carpet of bluebells. Out of the woods, an attractive hedge-lined unsurfaced lane weaves its way through high pastures, giving distant views of the White Peak plateau, Black Rocks and the cliffs of Crich Stand.

Bonsall

At the end of the lane, there is Bonsall, whose Perpendicular church tower and spire has been beckoning you onwards for some time. In the centre of this old lead mining village is a sloping market square with a 17th-century cross. The Kings Head Inn, built in 1677, overlooks the square, and is rumoured to be haunted.

The lane out of Bonsall takes you to the edge of an area of old mine shafts and modern-day quarries. Here you're diverted into the woods above the Via Gellia, a valley named after Philip Gell who built the road from the quarry to the Cromford Canal.

Those who wish can make a short diversion from the woodland path to see the Arkwright Mill and the canal in Cromford (see Walk 36). The main route swings north, back into the woods of the Derwent Valley, passing the high hamlet of Upperwood, where fleeting views of Matlock appear through the trees.

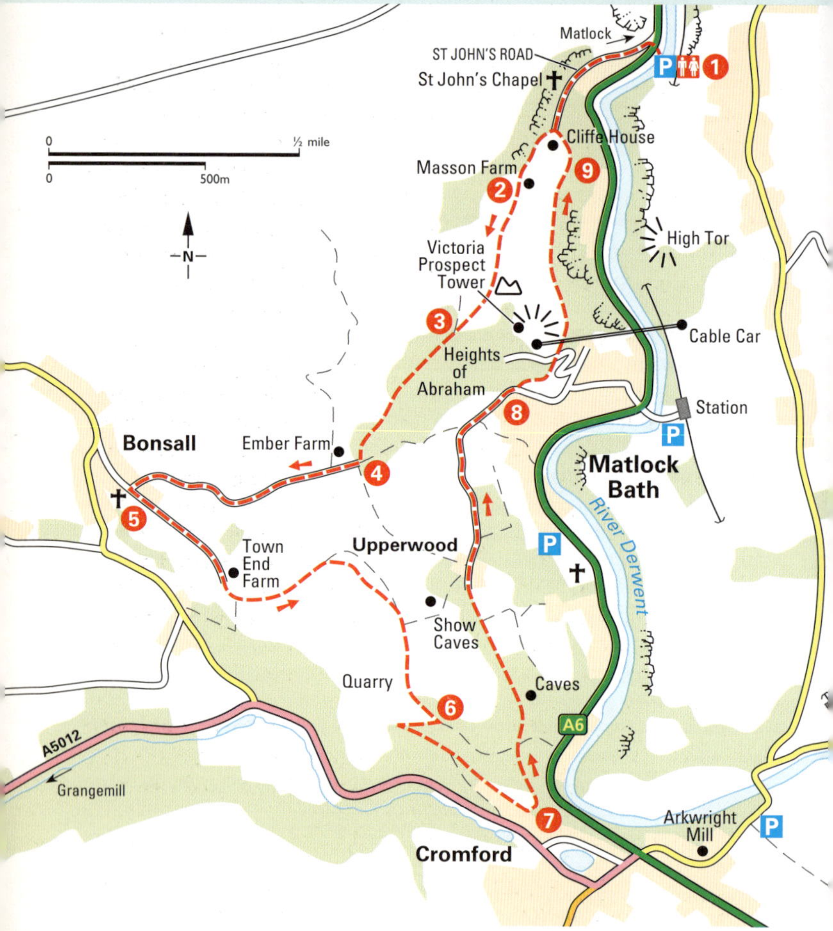

WALK 37 DIRECTIONS

1 Cross the A6 and then take St John's Road up the wooded slopes opposite. It passes beneath St John's Chapel to reach the gates of Cliffe House. Take the path on the right signposted 'Heights of Abraham'. The path climbs steeply upwards through the woods before veering left across the fields above Masson Farm.

WHILE YOU'RE THERE

Explore the Heights of Abraham by taking the alpine-style cable car, built in 1984. Included in the fare are the showcaves. There's also an interpretation centre and a restaurant in the complex.

2 Beyond the farmhouse and with Victoria Prospect Tower directly ahead, the waymarked path swings right and climbs up to the top of the field. Beyond this the footpath threads through hawthorn thickets before passing one of the entrances to the Heights of Abraham complex.

3 Ignore an obvious, engineered path and continue uphill along the perimeter of the complex and then turn left, going over a wall stile. After crossing a wide vehicle track the narrow footpath re-enters woodland.

4 At the far side of the woods, turn right on to a farm track close to Ember Farm. Join a pleasant lane that winds down pastured hill slopes into Bonsall village.

5 Turn left by the church along a lane that becomes unsurfaced when you get beyond Town End Farm. The lane finally comes to an abrupt end by the high fences of a quarry. Turn left here and follow a wide track around the perimeter of the quarry.

WHERE TO EAT AND DRINK

The Kings Head Inn at Bonsall is a fine old pub that is said to be haunted. They prepare very good bar meals here. Alternatively, you could try the Barley Mow on The Dale in Bonsall. This is a popular 17th-century inn with real ales and a reputation for serving excellent food.

6 Where the fence ends, continue down the track, bending sharply right then left along a narrow path through woodland high above the Via Gellia, then take the left fork after about 300yds (274m).

7 Turn left when you reach the next junction, following the footpath waymarked for the Derwent Valley Walk (DVW). This climbs further up the wooded bank, then turns left, tracing a mossy wall on the right. It rakes across the wooded hillside, passes above Cromford Court, then climbs away past some cave entrances to a lane at Upperwood. Ignore the next DVW sign and continue along the lane between cottages and past the West Lodge entrance to the Heights of Abraham showcave.

8 After 100yds (91m) leave the surfaced road for a stepped path, which goes through woods on the left, signed 'Matlock'. Climb some steps to reach a high wooden footbridge over the Heights of Abraham approach road, and then continue on the woodland path. You will pass under the Heights of Abraham cable cars before joining a farm track that comes in from the left.

9 This joins St John's Lane and the outward route at Cliffe House. Retrace your steps to the start.

WHAT TO LOOK OUT FOR

St John's Chapel was designed and built in 1897 by Sir Guy Dauber for Mrs Harris, who lived at Rock House. It was meant to serve the parishioners who found it difficult to reach St Giles at Matlock, but also it was a place for those worshippers who preferred a High Church service.

WALK 38

A Tissington Trail of Two Villages

Joining the famous trackbed of the Tissington Trail between the very different villages of Parwich and Tissington.

DISTANCE *4.25 miles (7km)* **MINIMUM TIME** *2hrs 30min*

ASCENT/GRADIENT *525ft (160m)* ▲▲▲ **LEVEL OF DIFFICULTY** +++

PATHS *Field paths, lanes and an old railway trackbed, lots of stiles*

LANDSCAPE *Village and rolling farm pastures*

SUGGESTED MAP *OS Explorer OL24 White Peak*

START/FINISH *Grid reference: SK 177522*

DOG FRIENDLINESS *Mostly on farmland, keep dogs on leads*

PARKING *Tissington Trail pay car park*

PUBLIC TOILETS *At car park*

The approach to Tissington is through a magnificent avenue of lime trees, and when you first see the place it completes the idyll of a perfect village. On one side of a huge green is Tissington Hall, the home of the Fitzherbert family since the reign of Elizabeth I: on the other a neat row of cottages and a slightly elevated Norman church. The trouble with Tissington is that it is too perfect, and to avoid the crowds you'll have to visit mid-week.

On this walk you save Tissington village for last, preferring instead to take to the Tissington Trail, the former trackbed of the Ashbourne-to-Buxton railway, which was closed by Dr Beeching in 1967. The route soon leaves the old track behind and descends into the valley of Bletch Brook, then out again on to a pastured hillside. Now you see Parwich, tucked in the next valley beneath a wooded hill. Overlooking the village is a fine 18th-century red-brick building, Parwich Hall.

Parwich

Parwich isn't as grand as Tissington, but it has a village green, and there is a duck pond too. At certain times of year, you may see moorhens and their young swimming about among the tangled irises. But Parwich is a more peaceful place and the winding lanes are almost traffic-free in comparison. St Peter's Church is Victorian, but incorporates the chancel arch, and a carved tympanum from the old Norman church.

Leaving Parwich behind, the path continues over the hillside, back into the valley of Bletch Brook and the Tissington Trail, then back for a better look at Tissington. If you go round the lane clockwise you will pass the Methodist chapel before coming to one of Tissington's five wells, the Coffin Well. Every year on Ascension Day Tissington's locals dress these wells. This involves making a clay-covered dressing frame on to which pictures are traced. Flower petals are then pressed into the clay, creating the elaborate patterns and pictures you see. The ceremony is unique to Derbyshire and the Peak District. Originally a pagan ceremony to appease the gods into keeping pure water flowing, it was later adopted by the Christian religion.

TISSINGTON

During the Black Death, when people from neighbouring villages were being ravaged by the plague, the Tissington villagers were kept in good health, due, they believe, to the pure water from the five wells.

Just past the Coffin Well there is a fine duck pond to admire, complete with a handful of ever-hungry ducks, but most eyes will be on the magnificent Jacobean hall. If it is closed to visitors, you can view it through the fine wrought iron gates built by Robert Bakewell, or get an elevated view from the churchyard.

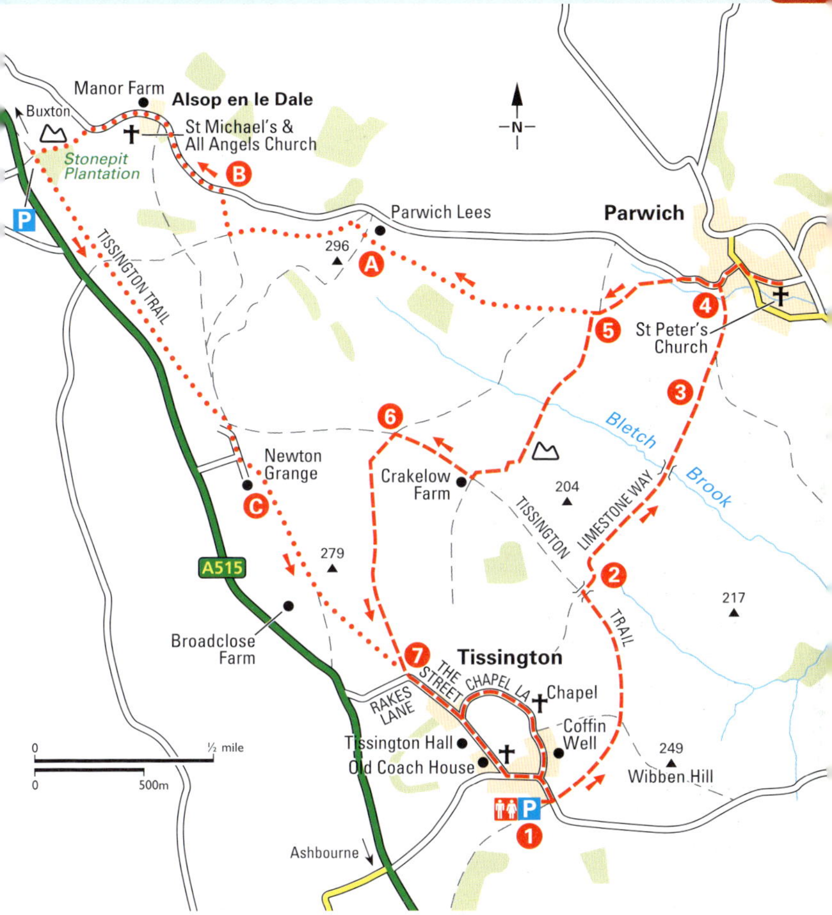

WALK 38 DIRECTIONS

1 From the Tissington Trail car park follow the trackbed of the north-east bound Tissington Trail (the former Ashbourne-to-Buxton railway). Ignore the first left turning and after about 800 yards (732m) take the path up and over the bridge to turn right on to a track.

2 Just past the first bend descend on the waymarked but trackless path into the valley of Bletch Brook, going through wide and sloping fields and across a footbridge spanning the brook itself. A more definite path establishes itself on the climb out of the valley. It reaches the top of a pastured spur, well to the right of a small barn.

3 In the next high field the path follows a hedge on the left to a stile in the field corner. It then descends to a footpath signpost, which points the short way across the last field to the western edge of the village.

4 For those who want to explore the village turn right, otherwise turn left down the lane to Brook Close Farm. A signposted footpath on the left slants up across the pathless slope to reach a stile into the next field. The path now heads south-westwards to the top right-hand corner of the field, then follows a muddy tree-lined track for a few paces.

WHILE YOU'RE THERE

Sir Richard Fitzherbert opens Tissington Hall to the public for guided tours during Easter week and specific dates in July and August. Visit www.tissington-hall.com for more details or pick up a leaflet from the local TIC.

5 On entering the next field turn left, follow a hedge on the left, then descend to recross Bletch Brook via a footbridge and not the gated concrete bridge nearby. It climbs up the middle of the next long field before zig-zagging up the steep upper slopes to reach the bridge over the Tissington Trail. Go down to the trail and turn right to follow it north-westwards.

WHAT TO LOOK OUT FOR

Many of the regularly ploughed fields of Parwich and Tissington will have few wild flowers in them, but take a look at the field-edges and the hayfields, for they will be rich in limestone-loving plants. In April and May, keep a watch for the increasingly rare cowslip (*Primula veris*). Its short single stem grows from a rosette of wrinkled leaves and its yellow flowers form a drooping cluster that can often be seen swaying in the breeze.

WHERE TO EAT AND DRINK

The Old Coach House tea rooms serves morning coffee, lunches and afternoon teas 11am–5pm. The Sycamore Inn in Parwich looks a little plain from the outside, but it serves good bar meals. The Bluebell Inn near the exit gates of the Tissington Estate has a good reputation for serving excellent bar meals.

6 After about 500yds (457m) turn left, following the unsignposted Tissington footpath over a stile to the top right-hand corner of a field. Now follow a wall on the right, all the way down to the edge of Tissington.

7 Go straight on along The Street to reach Chapel Lane. You can walk either way round the village square. The hall and church are straight ahead, while the Methodist chapel and the Coffin Well are on Chapel Lane to the left. The car park lies to the south-east of the square; take a left turn just beyond the Coffin Well.

An Extension to Alsop en le Dale

A slightly longer route discovers a third village, Alsop en le Dale, lying at the head of Bletch Brook's green vale.

See map and information panel for Walk 38

DISTANCE *6 miles (9.7km)* **MINIMUM TIME** *4hrs*

ASCENT/GRADIENT *558ft (170m)* ▲▲▲ **LEVEL OF DIFFICULTY** +++

WALK 39 DIRECTIONS (Walk 38 option)

There is more to walking in this area than the regimented furrow of the Tissington Trail, but it does make for easy navigation.

Follow Walk 38 to Point 5, but at the signpost beyond the muddy track at grid ref 182543, maintain a westerly direction, tracing the path towards Alsop en le Dale. The path runs parallel to Bletch Brook, passing through many fields and over many stiles en route.

Continue to follow the signposted route (Point A), aiming to the left of the house. The right of way traces the boundary wall, before descending to a stile hidden by hawthorns. Cross the lane beyond and continue west to the left corner of the next field.

Skirt the lower crag and tree-fringed slopes to the left before turning right on a stony cart track, which reaches the road just short of Alsop en le Dale (Point B).

Take the lane through the village, passing the Elizabethan Manor Farm, and St Michael's and All Angels Church. The church is Norman and the walls are an impressive 3ft (1m) thick.

Just beyond the next bend take the footpath climbing up the steep grassy hill slopes on the left to the woods of Stonepit Plantation. At the top turn left along the Tissington Trail.

After a mile (1.6km), descend some steps on the right and follow the lane towards Newton Grange Caravan Site (Point C). A footpath on the left bypasses the farmyard and continues south of south-east across several fields. Just beyond the small enclosure by Broadclose Farm the path, not particularly evident on the ground here, veers left, almost parallel to a power line. Beyond a fence corner (on the left) head for a stile in the far wall, then maintain direction across two small fields. The path emerges on Rakes Lane, north of Tissington village.

Take the lane into the village passing Tissington Hall, the church and the pond, as in Walk 38.

CARSINGTON RESERVOIR

Around Carsington Reservoir

Derbyshire's most controversial modern reservoir is now a magnet for wildlife.

DISTANCE *8 miles (12.9km)* **MINIMUM TIME** *4hrs*

ASCENT/GRADIENT *235ft (71m)* ▲▲▲ **LEVEL OF DIFFICULTY** +++

PATHS *Surfaced and unsurfaced waymarked paths, a few stiles*

LANDSCAPE *Reservoir, woodland and low pastured hillsides*

SUGGESTED MAP *OS Explorer OL24 White Peak*

START/FINISH *Grid reference: SK 241516*

DOG FRIENDLINESS *Severn Trent Water ask that dogs be kept on lead*

PARKING *Carsington Reservoir visitor centre pay car park*

PUBLIC TOILETS *At car park and Millfields*

WALK 40 DIRECTIONS

Planned in the 1960s and argued about well into the 1970s, Carsington Reservoir was finally inaugurated by the Queen in 1992. Built in a shallow valley with a poor catchment area, the reservoir's main supply is pumped from the River Derwent at Ambergate and conveyed 6.5 miles (10.4km) down a pipeline. When the Derwent's water levels are low, water is pumped in the opposite direction.

Severn Trent Water has built a state-of-the-art visitor centre, a sports and activity centre, a restaurant, shops and a sailing club. They boast about their good conservation policies and clean water. But somehow you get that sinking feeling as you cross the vast car park in search of a walk.

The gloom's short-lived however, for once you are past Millbank at the southern end of the reservoir, you will leave the tarmac behind and you start to see the wildlife – a swan, a moorhen, a grebe. And soon after that you are walking among wetlands and through woods, looking across the blue water to verdant hill slopes.

From the visitor centre follow the signposted bridleway southwards past the sailing club and across the huge dam, which holds back 7.8 billion gallons (35.5 billion litres) of water. When full the reservoir is 100ft (30m) deep covering an area the size of 700 football pitches.

At the far end of the dam the tarmac path reaches Millfields, where there is a refreshment kiosk (seasonal) and toilets. From

WHERE TO EAT AND DRINK

The Miners Arms is a pleasant 400-year-old pub with a large beer garden. It serves good sandwiches and bar meals. You can gaze across Carsington Water while you eat at the visitor centre's Mainsail Restaurant. It is licensed and serves morning coffee, pleasant lunches and afternoon teas.

here a path with orange footprint markers continues close to the reservoir shoreline, reacquainting itself with the bridleway on several occasions. After crossing a wooden walkway over wet ground the path comes to a tarmac lane by Upperfields Farm.

Turn left along the lane, then right at a gate, following a track, signposted to Hopton. The winding track dips and climbs high above the sinuous lake shore, passing through pastureland and into the shade of woodland.

The track turns left at the northern end of the lake, then left again parallel to the main road. Cross the busy road, before continuing along the track on the other side of the lake. This leads northwards into Hopton village, where you follow the lane into neighbouring Carsington.

The Miners Arms doesn't look much from the road, but in fact the front is at the back and it's a good looking pub with a handy beer garden.

Follow the signs left, past the pub car park, then left again along the lane behind the pub, going right past Wash Farm and ahead to the main road once more. Across the road, follow the left fork path, to Sheepwash car park.

Take the waymarked path between the metalled car park loop roads and continue south-west, by-passing the conservation area.

If you fancy doing some birding while you're here, there are a couple of signposted detours to waterside hides. The reservoir is quickly establishing itself as a haven for wildfowl. Wigeon, pochard and tufted ducks regularly winter here, while in the summer you will probably see great crested grebes. There are also many waders, including incongruous-seeming cormorants and elegant grey herons. The watchtower, which provides a good place for viewing the bird life, was built as an observation post during the Second World War.

Beyond the second hide the path meets, then joins the bridleway, but gives it the slip again to cut a corner round one of the inlets. The ways continue to flirt with each other like this until you reach the wildlife centre, where you should opt for the bridleway to take you back to the visitor centre.

WHILE YOU'RE THERE

The visitor centre has a fascinating exhibition demonstrating the value of water and the reliability of its quality. There's a water feature, the Kugel, where a 3ft (90cm) sphere of Bavarian granite revolves mysteriously on a socket. Water pumped from the socket, lubricates the sphere, allowing it to revolve on the slightest touch. On Stones Island there's a monument, cut from Derbyshire gritstone. It was designed by the landscape architect, Lewis Knight and erected in 1992.

WHAT TO LOOK OUT FOR

The American ruddy duck, which has a reddish back, white cheeks and large blue bill, is a regular on Carsington Water. The little duck escaped from the Wildlife Trust and is now threatening to overrun native species, such as the European white-headed duck.

WALK 41

Skeletons from the Past

Miners' tracks to the lead village of Brassington.

DISTANCE *5.5 miles (8.8km)* **MINIMUM TIME** *3hrs 30min*

ASCENT/GRADIENT *1,148ft (350m)* ▲▲▲ **LEVEL OF DIFFICULTY** +++

PATHS *Hill paths, some hard to follow, and railway trackbed, numerous stiles*

LANDSCAPE *Limestone hills*

SUGGESTED MAP *OS Explorer OL24 White Peak*

START/FINISH *Grid reference: SK 249528*

DOG FRIENDLINESS *Dogs on leads over farmland, can run free on long stretches of enclosed railway trackbed*

PARKING *Sheepwash pay car park by Carsington Reservoir*

PUBLIC TOILETS *None on route*

He was as lean as a skeleton, pale as a dead corpse, his hair and beard a deep black, his flesh lank, and, as we thought, something of the colour of lead itself.

So wrote Daniel Defoe on seeing a lead miner, who had been living in a cave at Harborough Rocks. In times past Carsington and Brassington lived and breathed lead. Prior to the construction of Carsington Reservoir, archaeologists discovered a Romano-British settlement here, which could have been the long-lost Ludutarum, which was the centre of the lead-mining industry in Roman times.

As you walk out of Carsington into the world of the miner, you're using the very tracks he would have used. But the lesions and pockmarks of the endless excavations are being slowly healed by time, and many wild flowers are beginning to proliferate in the meadows and on hillsides.

Brassington

Weird-shaped limestone crags top the hill, then Brassington appears in the next valley with its Norman church tower rising above the grey rooftops of its 17th- and 18th-century houses. Brassington's former post office used to be the tollhouse for the Loughborough turnpike. St James Church is largely Norman, though it was heavily restored in the late 19th century, including the north aisle, which was added in 1880. The impressive south arcade has fine Perpendicular windows. High on the inner walls of the Norman tower is a figure of a man with his hand on his heart. The carving is believed to be Saxon: the man, Brassington's oldest resident.

Climbing out of Brassington the route takes you over Hipley Hill, where there are more remnants of the mines, and more limestone outcrops. On the top you could have caught the train back, but the Cromford High Peak railway closed in 1967, so you are left with a walk along its trackbed. It's a pleasant walk though, through a wooded cutting, with meadow cranesbill and herb Robert thriving among trackside verges and crags.

Harborough Rocks beckon from the left. Archaeologists have uncovered evidence that sabre-toothed tigers, black bears and hyenas once sought the shelter of nearby caves. They also discovered relics and artefacts from Roman and Iron Age dwellers. For those with extra time, there's an entertaining path winding between the popular climbing crags to the summit, which gives wide views across the White Peak and the lowlands of the East Midlands. Carsington Reservoir is seen to perfection, surrounded by chequered fields, woods and low rounded hills. Leaving the railway behind, there's one last hill, Carsington Pasture, to descend before returning to the lake.

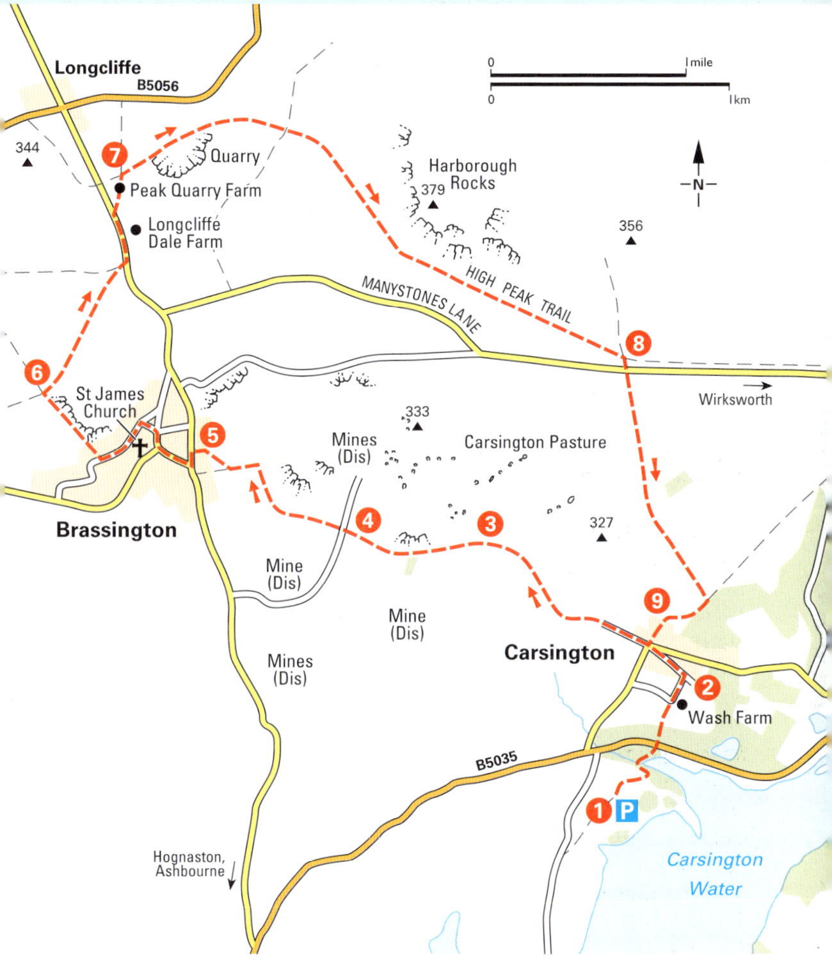

WALK 41 DIRECTIONS

1 Take the signposted path northwards towards Carsington. It winds through scrub woods and rounds a finger of the lake before reaching the B5035 road. The path continues on the other side, meeting a lane by Wash Farm and going straight on to enter the village by the Miners Arms.

2 Turn left along the lane to reach the Hopton road. Where the road turns left go straight ahead along a narrow lane passing several cottages. Beyond a gate the lane becomes a fine green track beneath the limestone-studded slopes of Carsington Pasture.

3 Where the track swings left you reach a gate; go through the gate then immediately fork right off the main path on a path climbing the grassy slopes to the west. At the top aim right of a copse and go through a gap in the broken wall before descending into a little valley.

4 Go over two stiles to cross a green lane, then follow a miners' track for 200yds (183m) towards some old mine workings. Here a footpath sign directs you around some limestone outcrops before arcing right towards Brassington. Turn left at the wall stile and follow the waymarked route across the fields into the village.

5 Turn left, then immediately right up Miners Hill. Now go right up Jasper Lane, left up Red Lion Hill, and left again along Hillside Lane. After 200yds (183m) leave the lane for a footpath on the right, which climbs past more limestone outcrops. The faint path gradually veers right, and passes the head of a green lane.

6 Here climb right over the pathless wall stile. Through the next three fields the path climbs parallel to, and to the right of, a line of wooden electricity pylons.

WHERE TO EAT AND DRINK

You can break the route for refreshment at Ye Old Gate Inn in Brassington, which serves Marstons ales. Children must be ten years old or over.

WHILE YOU'RE THERE

Take a look round Hognaston, an ancient Norse settlement dominated by its fine church dedicated to St Bartholomew. The church dates back to 1200 and has an ornate Norman doorway with a tympanium showing a bishop and his crook, with lambs and wild beasts. In medieval times the church tower with its 5ft (1.5m) thick walls was used as a defensive keep to protect the villagers' livestock.

In the fourth field bear half right above the rock outcrops and go through the top gate. Now aim for the extensive buildings of Longcliffe Dale Farm. After going over the next stile, turn left up the road, passing the farm. A footpath on the right then cuts a corner to the High Peak Trail, passing an electricity substation and Peak Quarry Farm.

7 Turn right along the trackbed of the High Peak Trail passing the Harborough Rocks.

8 Go right at the footpath signed to 'Carsington'. This path descends a small field to cross Manystones Lane. Follow the wall across Carsington Pasture, then descend by woods to a gate by a cottage.

9 Turn left down a little ginnel leading to the road and left again to retrace your earlier route back to Sheepwash car park.

WHAT TO LOOK OUT FOR

Despite their apparently sterile soil, the spoil tips have been colonised by a range of lead-tolerant plants, flourishing among the grassy heaps. You may see mountain pansy, spring sandwort, eyebright or autumn gentians.

Climbing up to Crich in Search of Cardale

On Crich Chase through TV-land to the monument of Crich Stand.

DISTANCE *7.5 miles (12.1km)* **MINIMUM TIME** *5hrs*

ASCENT/GRADIENT *721ft (220m)* ▲▲▲ **LEVEL OF DIFFICULTY** +++

PATHS *Woodland and field paths and canal tow path, many stiles*

LANDSCAPE *Woods and pastured hills*

SUGGESTED MAP *OS Explorer OL24 White Peak*

START/FINISH *Grid reference: SK 349517*

DOG FRIENDLINESS *Keep on lead across farmland, also by canal to protect the wildlife of nature reserve*

PARKING *Ambergate, car park by station*

PUBLIC TOILETS *At A6/A610 junction at start and at Crich near Black Swan*

The first five minutes of the walk are as uneventful as the rest is fascinating, and include such delights as a modern railway station and a busy road with heavy traffic. But as soon as you've turned the corner and crossed over Chase Bridge you're walking in a different world. An ivy-clad wall effectively blocks sight and sound of the road, the railway and the canal, tangled with irises and pondweed, ambles by slowly through the trees. Watch out for the bright yellow-and-black spotted longhorn beetle feeding on the meadowsweet and the holly blue butterflies in springtime.

Familiar to Millions

On this journey you save the greater part of the canal walking to the end, in order to climb through the woodland of Crich Chase, once part of a hunting forest owned by the 13th-century Norman baron, Hubert FitzRalph. After climbing high fields and along a gritstone edge, known as the Tors, you come upon Crich (pronounced so the 'i' rhymes with eye). If you get that déjà-vu feeling it's because Crich was *Peak Practice's* Cardale until the series moved to Longnor in 2001. Past the market cross and across more fields you come to the National Tramway Museum.

Back on track

The walk continues to its high point on Crich Stand, a limestone crag isolated by an area of gritstone. Capping the Stand is an impressive 60ft (19m) beacon tower, rebuilt in 1921 to commemorate the Sherwood Foresters killed in the two World Wars. On a clear day you can pick out Lincoln and its cathedral in the distance. Often you will see kestrels hovering around the cliff edge, searching for their prey.

The path descends through more woodland, beneath the shady gritstone cliffs of the old Dukes Quarry and down to the canal at Whatstandwell. The canal here has been allowed to silt up, and has become a haven for wildlife. It's well known for its many varieties of hoverfly, its azure damselflies and brown chinamark moths.

Wealth of Wildlife

Yellow irises and flowering rush, which has pink flowers, can be seen on the water's edge, while broad-leaved pondweed clogs the middle of the canal. That doesn't seem to impede the moorhens or mallards though. By the time you get back to Ambergate you will have seen a wealth of wildlife, but you can rest assured that much more wildlife will have seen you.

WALK 42 DIRECTIONS

1 Leave the car park at Ambergate Station and walk down the road under the bridge and then turn right along the busy A6. Turn right up Chase Road, which cuts underneath the railway bridge to the Cromford Canal. Follow the tow path northwards to the next bridge.

2 Go over the bridge before following a footpath climbing into the woodland of Crich Chase. In the upper reaches of the wood the waymarked path swings left; follow it to pass through some small clearings. It then follows a wall on the right at the top edge of the wood. Turn right over a stile, then climb across two fields to reach Chadwick Nick Lane.

3 Turn right along the road. After 300yds (274m) a path on the left begins with some steps and a stile, and continues the climb northwards across numerous fields with stiles and gates – and by the rock outcrops of The Tors.

WHILE YOU'RE THERE

Take time to visit the National Tramway Museum at Crich, where you can travel all day on vintage trams from all over the world. There's a period townscape, including the Georgian façade of Derby's old Market Place, which was relocated in 1972 after the Derby building was damaged by fire. There's also an all-day picture show. Staff are trained to help the disabled, and those with hearing or visual difficulties. Dogs are welcome in the museum. It's open daily from April to October.

4 The path becomes an enclosed ginnel, which emerges on Sandy Lane. Follow this to the Market Square, where you turn left, then right along Coasthill. Coasthill leads to an unsurfaced lane. Where the lane ends, follow a path in the same direction across fields to join another lane by some houses. Follow this to Carr Lane, then turn right, passing the entrance to the National Tramway Museum.

5 Continue along the road to a sharp right-hand bend, then turn left along the approach road to Crich Stand, topped by the Sherwood Foresters Monument. There's a small fee if you want to go up to the viewing platform on the monument, but otherwise continue along the public right of way on the right. The footpath, signed to Wakebridge and Plaistow, veers half right through shrubs and bramble, before circumnavigating Cliff Quarry.

WHERE TO EAT AND DRINK

The Hurt Arms at Ambergate is a popular family friendly pub that serves food daily, but for those with more sophisticated tastes, try the Black Swan by the Market Place in Crich.

WHAT TO LOOK OUT FOR

St Mary's Church was consecrated in 1135. It has a Perpendicular spired west tower with a Norman north arcade and a 14th-century chancel. Inside there is a circular Norman font, which is unusually large, and many tombs, including the one of Sir William de Wakebridge, whose family were wiped out by the plague.

6 The path then crosses over the museum's tram track near its terminus, before winding down the hillside through attractive scrub woodland. It joins a wide track that descends past Wakebridge and Cliff farms before coming to a road.

7 Turn right along the road for a few paces, then turn left on a footpath. This descends south across fields before swinging right to enter a wood. A well-defined path passes beneath quarried rockfaces, and crosses a minor road before reaching the canal at Whatstandwell.

8 Turn left and follow a most delightful tow path for 2 miles (3.2km) through the shade of tree boughs. At Chase Bridge you meet the outward route and retrace your steps back to the car park.

Dove Dale: Ivory Spires and Wooded Splendour

A gentle walk through the inspirational alpine-like splendour of the Peak's most famous dale.

DISTANCE *5 miles (8km)* **MINIMUM TIME** *3hrs 30min*

ASCENT/GRADIENT *557ft (170m)* ▲▲▲ **LEVEL OF DIFFICULTY** +++

PATHS *Mostly good paths, lanes, a few stiles, one steep scramble*

LANDSCAPE *Partially wooded dales, and high pastures*

SUGGESTED MAP *OS Explorer OL24 White Peak*

START/FINISH *Grid reference: SK 146509*

DOG FRIENDLINESS *Dogs should be kept under close control*

PARKING *Dovedale pay car park, near Thorpe*

PUBLIC TOILETS *At car park*

Right from the start there's drama as you follow the River Dove, wriggling through a narrow gorge between Bunster Hill and the towering pyramid of Thorpe Cloud. A limestone path urges you to climb to a bold rocky outcrop high above the river. Lovers' Leap has a fine view across the dale to pinnacles of the Twelve Apostles. It's a view to gladden your hearts – not the sort of place you'd think of throwing yourself from at all. However, in 1761 an Irish dean and his lady companion, who were out horse riding (or were they horsing about?) fell off the rock. The dean died of his injuries but the lady survived to tell the tale.

Spires and Caves

The Dove writhes round another corner. Above your heads, flaky fingers of limestone known as the Tissington Spires rise out from thick woodland cover. Just a few footsteps away on the right there's a splendid natural arch, which is just outside the entrance to Reynard's Cave. This is the result of the cave's roof collapsing.

The dale's limestone walls close in. The path climbs to a place more remote from the rushing river, which often floods around here. As the valley opens out again two gigantic rock stacks face each other across the Dove. Pickering Tor has a small cave at its foot. A little footbridge allows you across to the other side to the foot of Ilam Rock. This 80ft (25m) leaning thumb of limestone has an overhang on the south side that's popular with climbers. It too has a cave at the bottom, which is only 4ft (1.2m) at the entrance but opens out to over 30ft (10m) inside.

You will get a better view of them when you cross the little footbridge to the cave at the foot of the rocks. On this side you're in Staffordshire and the paths are less populated.

Hurt's Wood and Hall Dale

The walk into Hall Dale heralds a less formal landscape. The dale is dry and it climbs up the hillside. Hurt's Wood has wych elm, whitebeam, ash and rowan. Some fences have kept grazing animals out, allowing the trees and shrubs to regenerate. In Hurt's Wood is alive and well. You'll hear and see many birds – warblers, redstarts and blackcaps; and you'll see wild flowers – dog's mercury, wood anemone and wood forget-me-not.

It seems a shame to leave the dale behind but soon you're on a quiet lane with Ilam and the Manifold Valley on your right and a shapely peak, Bunster Hill, on your left. Cross the shoulder of the hill, then a ridge and furrow of a medieval field system, then back into the valley of the Dove.

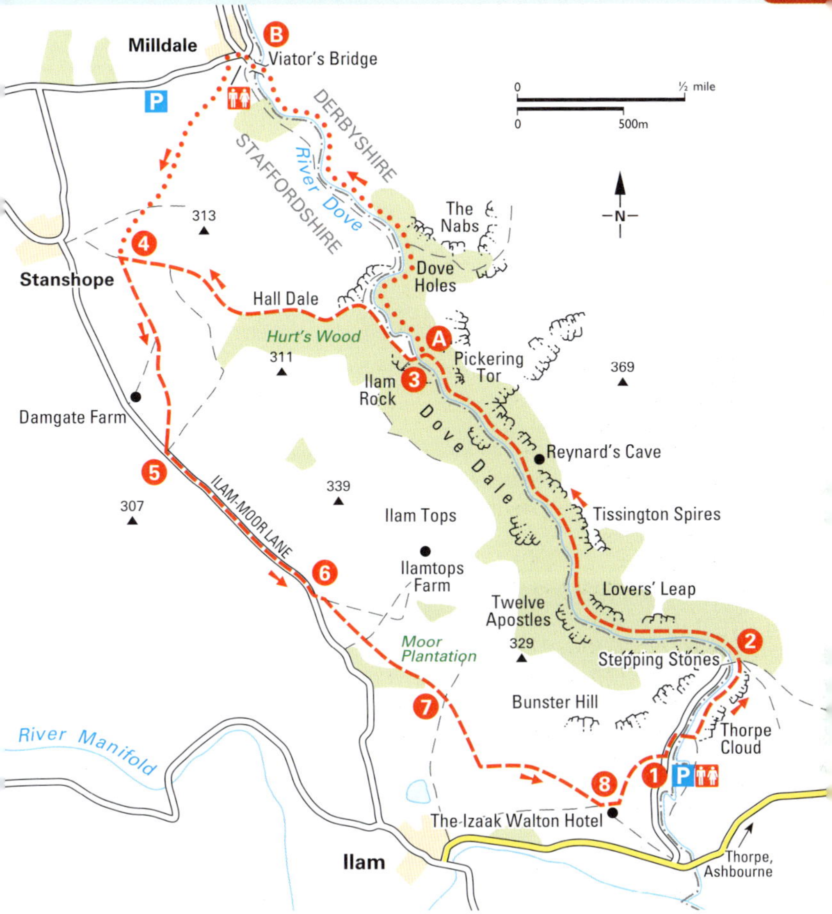

WALK 43 DIRECTIONS

1 Turn right out of the car park and follow the road along the west bank of the River Dove. Cross the footbridge to the opposite bank and turn left along a wide footpath. This path twists and turns through the narrow dale, between Bunster Hill and Thorpe Cloud.

2 Follow the path as it climbs some steps up through the woods on to the justifiably famous rocky outcrop of Lovers' Leap, then descends past the magnificent Tissington Spires and Reynard's Cave. Here a huge natural arch surrounds the much smaller entrance to the historic cave. As the dale narrows the path climbs above the river.

3 The dale widens again. Leave the main path for a route signposted 'Stanshope', and cross the footbridge over the Dove. A narrow woodland path turns right beneath the huge spire of Ilam Rock. Ignore the signposted turning for Ilam and follow the path as it swings left into Hall Dale. Following the valley bottom, it climbs out of the woods into a rugged limestone-cragged gorge.

4 As the gorge shallows the path enters pastureland – the village of Stanshope is on the skyline. At a crossroads of paths (grid ref 130541) turn left through a squeeze stile in the wall and head south with a wall on the right. Where the wall turns right, keep straight ahead to another stile, and then veer half right by a wall in the next field. The path cuts diagonally to the left across the last two fields to reach Ilam Moor Lane, 250yds (229m) south of Damgate Farm.

WHERE TO EAT AND DRINK

The Dovedale Bar at The Izaak Walton Hotel, near the start/finish of this walk, is open all day for food and drink and welcomes walkers. There's even a 'boot shed' for muddy footwear.

5 Turn left to walk along the quiet country lane. From here, there are magnificent views from here down to Ilam and the Manifold Valley ahead of you and down to the right.

6 After 800yds (732m) take a footpath on the left, following a drive for a few paces before turning right over a stile. A field path, now heads south-east, traversing low grassy fellsides to the top of Moor Plantation woods.

WHILE YOU'RE THERE

It will be tempting to climb to the top of Thorpe Cloud, for the sharp summit has wonderful views, both down the dale and across the expansive flatlands of the Midlands. The path leaves the main route at Dovedale's meeting with Lin Dale. It rakes across the east flanks before doubling back north-west along the steep crest to the summit. You will have to return the same way.

7 Here the path (fallen away in places) cuts across the steep sides of Bunster Hill, before straddling its south spur and descending to cross a step-stile in the intake wall. A path now descends south-east across sloping pastures to the back of The Izaak Walton Hotel.

8 Turn left (north-east) by the hotel across more fields and back to the car park.

WHAT TO LOOK OUT FOR

The Dove is a clear, pure river with lots of wildlife both in and around the water. Brown trout and grayling feed on the caddis flies and mayflies, while you may see a kingfisher diving for a minnow or bullhead.

Dove Dale, Viator's Bridge and Milldale

A slightly longer route takes you to Izaak Walton's famous bridge.

See map and information panel for Walk 43

DISTANCE *6 miles (9.7km)* **MINIMUM TIME** *4hrs*
ASCENT/GRADIENT *623ft (190m)* ▲▲▲ **LEVEL OF DIFFICULTY** +++

WALK 44 DIRECTIONS (Walk 43 option)

To complete the Dove Dale tour you really should take in the lovely little side valley of Milldale, made famous by Izaak Walton, and worth a visit in its own right.

Follow Walk 43 through Dove Dale to Point 3, but this time stay with the east bank when passing Pickering Tor. The path follows the S-shaped curve of the dale beneath Dove Holes (Point A). The cavities were cut by the river before it wore its way down to its present level.

The next stretch of river passes over a series of impressive weirs, then the valley makes one more twist to reveal a little twin-arched packhorse bridge ahead.

It's called Viator's Bridge (Point B), a name that comes from Izaak Walton's *Compleat Angler*, where the bridge is remembered in the Viator's Tale. On arriving at the bridge the jagger, Viator, moans to his sidekick, Piscator, 'Why a mouse can hardly go over it: 'Tis not two fingers broad'.

Cross the bridge over to the west bank, then turn right past the National Trust information barn and toilets into Milldale. Here a cluster of houses and a shop huddle into the sheltered gorge. The shop has a refreshment kiosk for drinks and hot pies, and on busy days you'll see walkers eating their sandwiches by both the roadside and the river bank.

Turn left up the road, then left again after about 150yds (137m) on a signposted footpath, climbing left of a cottage and up through a mini ravine. In summer the footpath can be a little overgrown in places. After passing through several squeeze stiles the path heads south-west across fields. In the second field there's a dry-stone wall for guidance. It's on the left for two fields, then, beyond another stile you change over to the other side.

Where the path joins a grassy track, Pasture Lane, turn right along it for about 200yds (183m), then turn left on another signposted field path. This descends south-west, joining the Hall Dale path from Walk 43 at a crossroads of paths (above Point 4). Follow the instructions for Walk 43 from here on.

Overleaf: Dove Dale, Peak District National Park (Walks 43 & 44)

PUBLIC
FOOTPATH ONLY
MILLDALE
& DOVEDALE

WALK 45

Derby City

Derbyshire's bustling city is often overlooked, on this linear route discover the city's many historic and fascinating nooks and crannies.

DISTANCE 3 miles (4.8km) **MINIMUM TIME** 2hrs
ASCENT/GRADIENT Negligible ▲▲▲ **LEVEL OF DIFFICULTY** +++
PATHS Surfaced riverside path and town streets
LANDSCAPE Cityscape
SUGGESTED MAP OS Explorer 259 Derby
START Grid reference: SK 377345 **FINISH** Grid reference: SK 354365
DOG FRIENDLINESS Can run free in park and along some riverside paths
PARKING Alvaston Park car park
PUBLIC TOILETS Alvaston Park
NOTE Arriva buses 40, 41, 44 and 45 run regularly between Derby and Alvaston Park

WALK 45 DIRECTIONS

In 1724 Daniel Defoe wrote, 'Derby… is a town of gentry rather than trade; with a fine town-house and very handsome streets'. But the coming of the railway in 1838 changed all that. By the end of the 19th century Derby was the major railway manufacturing town of England.

A walk in Derby by the banks of the River Derwent, gives you some insight into its continuing change. Many of the railway sites have been redeveloped or left to return to nature.

From the car park go round the right side of the large lake. On reaching the river turn left, following the tarmac riverside path under the railway bridge. On this section of the river you could well see a grey heron or a cormorant standing ever so still, waiting for its fish supper. On your left now is the modern retail development of Pride Park, which was the former site of locomotive and railway engineering works, but now includes the Derby County football stadium.

As you approach the city centre, the path goes under Five Arches railway bridge, built by Robert and George Stephenson. Just beyond the bridge you cross Mill Fleam where you may see freshwater crayfish, which look like very small lobsters. They're now quite rare, due to pollution.

WHERE TO EAT AND DRINK

You're spoilt for choice in Derby. Eating places range from an outdoor kiosk selling bacon sandwiches to high class French restaurants. Perhaps one of the most handily located establishments is Derby Cathedral Centre coffee shop, opposite the cathedral entrance on Iron Street. Part of the cathedral gift shop, it's open Monday to Saturday and sells a wide range of snacks, drinks and light refreshments.

The riverside path now skirts a small open park, on the former site of Holmes Copper Rolling and Slitting Mills. It continues under Holmes road bridge, through the Riverside Gardens, across Derwent Street and into Cathedral Green and the recently redeveloped waterfront.

WHILE YOU'RE THERE

The Royal Crown Derby porcelain company celebrated its 250th anniversary in the year 2000. The visitor centre on Osmaston Road shows you the skills of making bone china that have been handed down through the generations of their craftsmen. It's open seven days a week and operates a factory tour each weekday.

Look out for the statue of Bonnie Prince Charlie, the work of Anthony Stones, unveiled in 1995. Continue past Derby's Museum of Industry and History. It occupies the site of Sir Thomas Lombe's silk mill, the first of its kind in England. The original mill was destroyed by fire in 1910 – only the octagonal tower and the foundation arches remain.

The path passes beneath the modern inner ring road bridge before continuing to St Mary's, an 18th-century bridge that replaced a 13th-century one. At road above the bridge you will see the 15th-century Catholic Chapel of St Mary on the Bridge.

The walk through city streets now begins. Turn left down Sowter Road, take the first right (St Michaels Lane) on to Queen Street, where you turn left to pass the 16th-century timber-framed Dolphin Inn. Just beyond is the Cathedral of All Saints, which has a magnificent 212ft (65m) Perpendicular tower. Inside, there's an elaborate wrought-iron chancel screen built by Robert Bakewell, and the 17th-century marble tomb of Elizabeth, Countess of Shrewsbury – better known as Bess of Hardwick.

Turn right down St Mary's Gate, then left along Bold Lane. Go right along Cheapside for a there-and-back walk to see Friar Gate, a fine Georgian street, which includes architect Joseph Pickford's house, now a museum.

Returning to Bold Lane, head down Sadler Gate where many 16th-century houses are masked by 18th-century façades. In 1745 the Lloyds Bank building, at the corner of Sadler Gate and Iron Gate, was commandeered by Bonnie Prince Charlie's army after a triumphant march into Derby. Unfortunately for the Young Pretender, local support had deserted him. As the Duke of Devonshire had assembled a huge defensive army, Bonnie Prince Charlie was forced to retreat.

After turning right down Iron Gate, go left into the Market Place, through the old Guildhall and the Victorian Market Hall. Go straight on along Exchange Street and left up East Street to the bus stops.

WHAT TO LOOK OUT FOR

The present St Mary's Bridge in Derby was built in 1794, though there has been a bridge on this site since 1275. By its side is a bridge chapel, built around 1450 and one of only five that survive in England today. Beneath the chapel you'll see another stone arch. This is part of the previous medieval bridge.

WALK 46

Osmaston and Shirley Parks

To the south of the Peak District National Park, two aristocratic estates provide gentle parkland walking.

DISTANCE *4.5 miles (7.2km)* **MINIMUM TIME** *3hrs 30min*
ASCENT/GRADIENT *295ft (90m)* ▲▲▲ **LEVEL OF DIFFICULTY** +++
PATHS *Estate tracks and field paths, quite a few stiles*
LANDSCAPE *Park, woodland and farm pasture*
SUGGESTED MAP *OS Explorer 259 Derby*
START/FINISH *Grid reference: SK 200435*
DOG FRIENDLINESS *Dogs should be on lead*
PARKING *Osmaston village hall car park*
PUBLIC TOILETS *None on route*

Osmaston is barely a few winding country lanes away from the buzzing traffic of Ashbourne, but it's just the unspoiled tranquil village you'd hope to find on a country walk. The moment you leave the car you will experience the slow tick-over of the place.

Mock Tudor

St Martin's Church was built in 1845 to replace a much earlier one. The parish register goes back to 1606. It's full of references to the Wright family, who for a long time were the local gentry and benefactors to the village. Francis Wright, the owner of the Butterley Iron Works, had Osmaston Hall built here in 1849. The hall itself was a mock-Tudor mansion and the gardens were landscaped. There's a memorial to him found in Ashbourne's Market Place.

In 1964 the hall's owner, Sir John Walker, decided to demolish the place when he moved to Okeover and took the Okeover family name. However, the grounds, Osmaston Park, are criss-crossed by rights of way, which make a pleasing itinerary for the walker.

Across the road from the car park is a terrace of four thatched cottages, built to celebrate the coronation of King George VI. As you walk down the lane you pass the Shoulder of Mutton, a fine village pub with much promise for the end of the day, then some more of those thatched cottages, this time built with rustic tawny-coloured local bricks. These cottages are much older than the ones seen earlier and they're timber framed.

At the end of the lane there's a duck pond. Even the ducks seem less noisy in Osmaston. The walk enters the woodlands of Osmaston Park and threads between two of the estate's many lakes. On the other side there's an old mill, built in the style of an Austrian chalet and complete with a waterwheel. The path climbs though more woodland.

Shirley's another pretty village with its own aristocracy – Earl Ferrers and the Shirley family. Viscount Tamworth, the heir to Earl Ferrers, still lives in the village. From Shirley the walk turns back across fields and woods to Osmaston Park, reaching another of the estate's lakes. This one has the best setting, with a lush meadow surround and the occasional heron.

Towering in the Woods

As you continue along the track, heading north and back into the woods now, you'll see a peculiar-looking tower peeping out from the canopy of trees. It's 150ft (45m) tall and all that remains of Osmaston Hall. The tower was designed to accommodate all the hall's various chimneys in one single stack. With this odd sight still lingering in your thoughts the walk ends in fine 'lord of the manor' style as you walk down the hall's main drive, saluted by a fine avenue of lime trees.

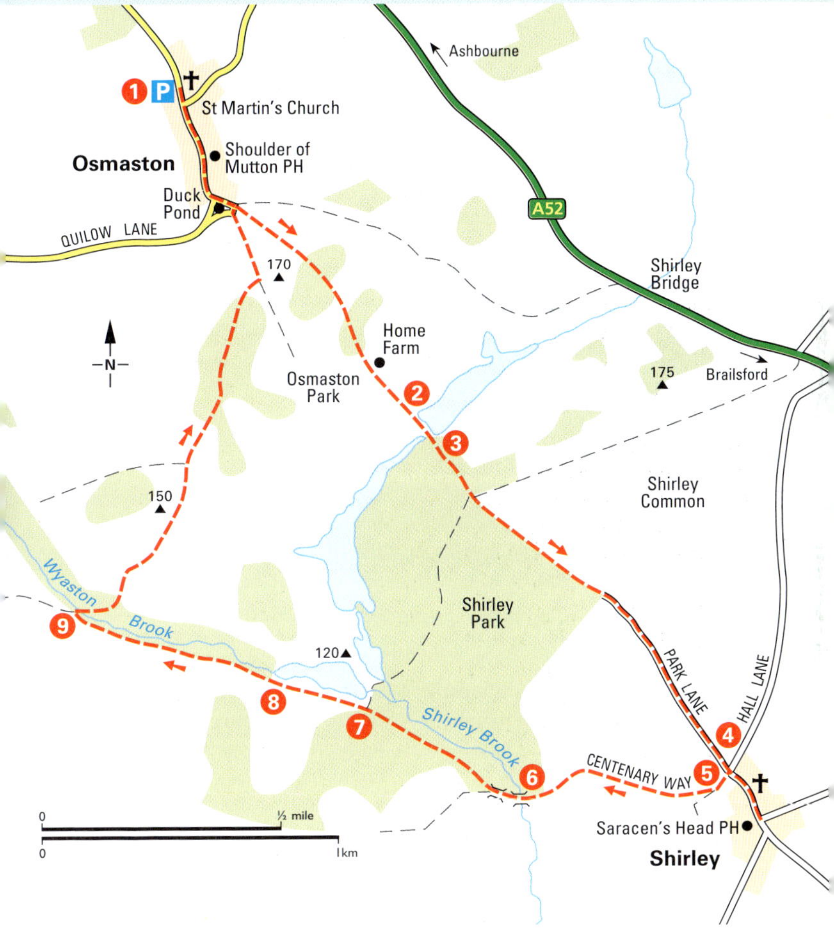

WALK 48 DIRECTIONS

❶ Turn right out of the Osmanton Village Hall car park and follow the road past the Shoulder of Mutton pub to the village green and duck pond. Turn left and then take the middle of three rights of way – marked 'Bridleway to Shirley'. The track descends among fields and through attractive woodland. Continue on the track past Home Farm, which lies to the left.

2 Follow the track it as it separates the two narrow lakes, to walk between them.

3 After passing an old watermill keep to the track ahead, which climbs up through the woodlands of Shirley Park. The track eventually becomes a tarmac lane, continuing towards Shirley.

4 The return path to Osmaston, highlighted by a Centenary Way (CW) waymarker, begins on the right, just before the village, but most walkers will want to take a look around the centre, if only for refreshment at the Saracen's Head.

WHILE YOU'RE THERE

Ashbourne proclaims itself to be the gateway to Dovedale. It has some fine old coaching inns. St Oswald's Church, with its 200ft (61m) plus spire and early 13th-century chancel, was described by George Eliot as 'the finest mere parish church in the kingdom'.

5 Return to the previously mentioned footpath, which begins with some steps. Beyond a stile it crosses a fenced-off section of lawn, previously part of a garden belonging to the cottage on the left. Beyond a second stile the path follows a hedge on the left round the edge of three fields. It cuts diagonally across a fourth field to a stile, beyond which you turn left to descend towards a wood, which is the southern extremity of Shirley Park.

6 Go over the footbridge to cross Shirley Brook and then follow a muddy streamside path to another footbridge. Go over this and then turn right into the woods on a path, which has another CW marker.

WHAT TO LOOK OUT FOR

The lakes are frequented by many birds, including grey heron, mallards, moorhens and many migratory wildfowl. The annual show of the Ashbourne Shire Horse Society is held in Osmaston Park in August.

7 Beyond a gate at the edge of the woods, ignore the CW path on the right. Instead, leave the woods and continue along a grassy sunken track heading across the pasture ahead and alongside a pleasant lake, the southernmost of the Osmaston Park lakes.

8 Where the track fades, maintain direction alongside the lake and then a narrow strip of woodland. You are walking through the valley of Wyaston Brook and, although the path is invisible on the ground, the stiles in the cross-fences are all in place.

9 The bridleway from Wyaston Grove joins the route just beyond one of these stiles (grid ref 196423). Double-back right along it, passing some railings on the right. The bridleway track now climbs north-east out of the valley and back into the estate of Osmaston Park. It becomes a tarmac drive and eventually turns left on to an avenue of lime trees, emerging by the village green. Turn left, by the duck pond, then right, back to the car park.

WHERE TO EAT AND DRINK

If you're after a traditional Sunday lunch try the Shoulder of Mutton at Osmaston, a free house with real ales. The Saracen's Head at Shirley serves excellent food if you're partial to a refreshment break in the middle of your walk.

Mackworth and Markeaton: a Rural Idyll

Very different from the austerity of the Peak District, this slice of South Derbyshire belongs more to the Midlands than the North.

DISTANCE *6 miles (9.7km)* **MINIMUM TIME** *4hrs*

ASCENT/GRADIENT *197ft (60m)* ▲▲▲ **LEVEL OF DIFFICULTY** +++

PATHS *Farm tracks and field paths, can be muddy after rain, quite a few stiles*

LANDSCAPE *Pastoral*

SUGGESTED MAP *OS Explorer 259 Derby*

START/FINISH *Grid reference: SK 333379*

DOG FRIENDLINESS *Dogs can run free in the park away from the playgrounds and along early stretches of riverside path*

PARKING *Markeaton Park pay car park*

PUBLIC TOILETS *Markeaton Park*

Markeaton Park's a bustling place in summer, but as soon as you cross the road and take the lane up to Markeaton Stones Farm you leave that all behind to enter a new rural world. The farmhouse is pristine, made from that warm-red local brick. The lawns, cottage gardens and stables show further that this place has been cared for.

It was summer when I walked this route, and the track wended its way through fields of wheat that was swaying with the wind and crackling in the heat of the sun. The aura of the place brought Gray's *Elegy* to mind, though the ploughman didn't plod his weary way home, he chugged down the path in his shiny green tractor, just shipped in from Japan.

As you climb the hill towards a stand of trees, look back and see Derby spread before you. Prominent in the view are the university, with its rooftop masts, and the cathedral, which dwarfs everything around it. The beeches of Vicar Wood guide you past the farm of the same name to the other side of the hill, where you can see mile upon mile of rolling farmland. Just beyond some trees lies the landscaped parklands of the estate, down to the hall and All Saints Church. Famous Scottish architect, Robert Adam, built the present hall for Nathanial Curzon in 1759.

A World Apart

A short stretch of road leads to the next cross-field section. Though the walking is a little rougher, it's still pleasantly pastoral. There's a lake in a shady hollow to the right and Bowbridge Fields Farm is a fine 19th-century, three-storey, red-brick building. As you reach the busy A52 there's a brief return to the present day, but Mackworth village is a surprise. It's only yards from the A52, but again, it's a world apart.

A tidy row of 17th- and 18th-century cottages lines an undulating, slightly twisted lane. In the middle is a Gothic stone-built gatehouse, the remains of Mackworth Castle, which was built around 1495 for the de Mackworth family, and destroyed in the Civil War. At the end of the lane is the church of All Saints, a rather austere 14th-century building with a Perpendicular tower. The last mile of the route follows the Bonnie Prince Charlie Walk across fields and back to the civilisation of Markeaton Park.

WALK 47 DIRECTIONS

1 Leave the car park at Markeaton Park and cross the road to follow a surfaced lane to Markeaton Stones Farm. When you're past the farm the track becomes a stony one, climbing gently around crop growing fields until you reach a T-junction.

2 Here turn left and then follow a crumbling tarmac lane up past a stand of trees until you reach the buildings of Upper Vicarwood Farm.

3 At the farm buildings continue through a gate on the left-hand side of the stable block and follow a grassy hilltop track.

4 Through a gate the track reaches Lodge Lane. Turn left along the lane to the gardens of Meynell Langley, then left again into a field next to the entrance to the drive. The path follows a hedge on the right. Through a small, wooded enclosure a lake appears in a hollow to the right. Beyond the next stile the route enters a large field and the hedge wanders off to the right.

5 Aim for a large lime tree at the far side of the field to find the next stile. Cross the footbridge spanning Mackworth Brook. The path now goes parallel to a hedge on the right, aiming for a large barn on the hillside ahead.

6 On reaching a gateway the path divides. Take the one to the left, whose direction is highlighted by a waymarking arrow. Go through the next gate and follow the right field-edge, passing to the left of the fine red-brick Bowbridge Fields Farm. Now head south across fields following a hedge on the left.

7 After going over a stile in a tall hedge, turn left along the pavement of the busy A52 (take care), passing a garage. After 600yds (549m) go left along Jarveys Lane passing through Mackworth village.

8 Where the lane turns sharp right, leave it for a path passing in front of the church. Bonnie Prince Charlie waymarks show the well-defined route eastwards across fields to Markeaton.

9 On reaching the road you can either turn left back to the car park or go straight ahead through Markeaton Park. For the latter go through the gateway, turn left over the twin-arched bridge spanning the lake, left by the children's playground, and left again past the boating lake.

WHILE YOU'RE THERE

You've seen Kedleston Hall through the trees, but it's worth seeing it properly, once you've taken off your boots. Designed by Robert Adam, it's set in parklands with lakes, cascades and woodland. There's a marble hall; an Indian Museum with objects collected by Lord Curzon while he was Viceroy of India; and an exhibition of original Robert Adam drawings. The hall is open afternoons between March and October.

WHERE TO EAT AND DRINK

For well-earned refreshment at the end of the walk visit the Markeaton Village Tea Rooms at Home Farm, near the gateway entrance to Markeaton Park. This new educational farm and visitor centre offers a range of light refreshments and is open Thursday to Sunday throughout the year and daily in summer. For bar and restaurant meals try the Mackworth Hotel.

WHAT TO LOOK OUT FOR

Have a look around Mackworth church. The exterior is quite plain and there have been tales that it had a defensive purpose. In contrast is the rather elaborate Victorian modification to the interior, including an elaborate, carved alabaster lectern and an alabaster slab commemorating Thomas Touchet.

Calke Abbey: The House that Time Forgot

Around Sir John Harpur's forgotten baroque mansion on Derbyshire's southern border.

DISTANCE *4 miles (6.4km)* **MINIMUM TIME** *2hrs*
ASCENT/GRADIENT *197ft (60m)*▲▲▲ **LEVEL OF DIFFICULTY** +++
PATHS *Estate roads and field paths, a few stiles*
LANDSCAPE *Parkland and crop fields*
SUGGESTED MAP *OS Explorer 245 The National Forest*
START/FINISH *Grid reference: SK 353241*
DOG FRIENDLINESS *On leads through farmland and abbey grounds*
PARKING *Village Hall car park, Ingleby Lane, Ticknall*
PUBLIC TOILETS *At car park*

Calke is not an abbey at all. The Augustinian order of monks did build one here in 1133 and dedicated it to St Giles, but since 1622 it has been the family home of the Harpurs and Harpur-Crewes.

In 1703 Sir John Harpur had the present baroque mansion built on the site of the abbey, keeping some of the old 6ft (2m) walls. This was a high society family, but things started to go wrong in the 1790s when Sir Henry Harpur took a lady's maid as his bride. Society shunned the couple and they, in turn, shunned society – the beginning of a tale of eccentricity and reclusiveness that would span two centuries.

Calke was a grand house with many rooms, and here was a family with money. When they tired of one room, they would just leave it the way it stood and move to another. For instance, when Sir Vauncey Harpur Crewe took a bride in 1876, he locked up his bachelor room, along with the heads of stuffed deer he had shot as a youth. When the National Trust bought the house in 1985 they found a dust-laden, neglected, but intriguing place, filled with treasures of centuries gone by.

Ticknall

Ticknall is an interesting village. Passing through it you see some pleasing timber-framed red brick cottages. When you reach the gates of the abbey, you are confronted with a horseshoe-shaped bridge, arching over the road. Built in 1800, it was part of an old tramway system, which included a 137yd (125m) tunnel under the main drive to the abbey. Limestone from Ticknall's brickworks used to be carried by horse-drawn trams to the canal at Willesley. On the return journey the load would have been coal. The scheme was abandoned in 1915, now just the bridge remains.

The tree-lined drive sets the scene for this trip round Calke. There are fallow deer in the woods, as well as barn and tawny owls. Betty's Pond is the first of the several lakes passed on the route. The house, being in a dip, hides until the last moment. Its magnificent three-storey south front has a four-column Ionic portico. If the place is open, inside you'll find a resplendent Gold Drawing Room and an 18th-century Chinese state bed.

A Grand Return

The route heads north to Mere Pond, which is full of lilies and surrounded by attractive mature woods. It reaches its highest point on the fields of White Lees. Here you get glimpses of the picturesque Staunton Harold Reservoir, built in 1964 to provide Leicester and the East Midlands with water, before you return to Ticknall.

WALK 48 DIRECTIONS

1 Turn right out of the car park and follow the road to its junction with the A road through the village. Turn left by the Wheel public house, then right by the bridge to go through the gates of the Calke Abbey Estate. The tarmac estate road goes between an avenue of mature lime trees and through the Middle Lodge Gates, where car drivers are charged to enter the grounds.

2 Continue south-east along the road, past Betty's Pond (left), then, as the road swings left, carry on along the grassy track towards the south end of the park.

WHERE TO EAT AND DRINK

The National Trust tea room at Calke Abbey, which serves drinks, snacks and main meals, is handily placed on the route and you don't have to pay to enter the house or gardens to access it.

3 By a white gate turn sharply left for a grassy track towards the abbey, which appears in a dip ahead. Turn left at the railings. After viewing the fine house, continue along the track past the red-brick stables and offices. Enter the large, grassy car park at the back and turn left for a path in the far corner. Go over a stile by an interpretation board and down steps to reach Mere Pond, a narrow strip of water surrounded by trees.

4 Turn right along a water's-edge path, then left between the end of the mere and the western extremities of another one, to climb through woodland to the north.

WHAT TO LOOK OUT FOR

By Ticknall's 19th-century church you can see the remains of a medieval church, St Thomas a Beckett's, which had become too small. The old church was so strong that it had to be blown up with gunpowder.

5 On meeting the track at the top edge of the woods, turn left for a few paces, then right through a gate. After tracing the wall on the left, go over a stile in the hedge ahead to enter the next field. The path now heads north of north-west along the left edge of crop fields, passing close to White Leys Farm. Just past a large ash tree, cross over a stile on the left and follow a field-edge track through more crop growing fields with the hedge on your right.

6 On meeting a flinted works road turn left, following it through an area of woodland and old gravel pits (now transformed into pretty wildlife ponds). The winding track passes several cottages and meets the A514 about 500yds (457m) to the east of the village.

7 Turn left along the road through the village, then right by the side of the Wheel pub to get back to the car park.

WHILE YOU'RE THERE

Seeing nearby Melbourne is a must. Neat Georgian houses crowd round the Monument in the Market Place. There's a short history of the town engraved on a bronze plaque. The Parish Church of St Michael and St Mary is far grander than you would expect for such a small town. This church, however, was built in the first half of the 12th century for the Bishops of Carlisle, who wanted to be as far away as possible from their troubled Border Country. For more information on Melbourne Hall (see Walk 49).

A Melbourne Extension

Good paths connect Calke Abbey with is neighbouring great house.

See map and information panel for Walk 48

DISTANCE *7.5 miles (12.1km)* **MINIMUM TIME** *3hrs 30min*

ASCENT/GRADIENT *460ft (140m)* ▲▲▲ **LEVEL OF DIFFICULTY** +++

WALK 49 DIRECTIONS (Walk 48 option)

If you are visiting Calke Abbey it makes sense to see neighbouring Melbourne Hall, originally a rectory for 12th-century Bishops of Carlisle, but substantially rebuilt by the Coke family in the 18th century.

Follow Walk 48 past Point 5 to the large ash tree (grid ref 366236 – Point A). Here, turn right and descend to cross one of Staunton Harold Reservoir's feeder streams. Ascend diagonally right across the next field, a lane and more fields to the right of Derby Hills House Farm. With the reservoir on your right, follow the waymarks past the newly planted Broadstone Holt Wood, part of the emerging National Forest (you will see other new plantations later on).

Aim for a lookout tower near the reservoir's visitor centre car park (Point B). Continue with the narrow path down to the road at Shaw House. Turn right, then left at the T-junction and walk past the Melbourne Arms.

After 100yds (91m), take the footpath on the right, traversing meadows above The Pool. The path curves left between houses to reach Penn Lane. Turn right on the lane to the end, then right again for Melbourne Hall (Point C).

From The hall go back up Church Street to the Market Place (Point D), then turn left along High Street, returning to the Melbourne Arms before turning right along Robinson's Hill.

Where this path meets the B587 road, go straight ahead along the Riding Bank bridleway. At the lane's end continue ahead, and alongside a field edge. The path gradually arcs left, past St Brides Farm to cross the end of a farm track. Go straight ahead and follow the field-edge (on the left), to come to the A514.

Across the road take the track past the newly planted Vees Wood into Robin Wood, where you turn left along a muddy path. At the southern edge of the wood maintain your direction across fields, keeping Ticknall's church spire to the south-west.

Go through the gate at the edge of the village, then turn right to continue along Chapel Street, which comes out on to the road opposite to the car park.

WALK 50

Trent Lock and Attenborough Reserve

Along the waterfront and into neighbouring Nottinghamshire.

DISTANCE *9.5 miles (15.3km)* **MINIMUM TIME** *5hrs 30min*

ASCENT/GRADIENT *Negligible* ▲▲▲ **LEVEL OF DIFFICULTY** +++

PATHS *Canal tow path, easy riverside and lakeside paths and tracks*

LANDSCAPE *Riverside and wetland*

SUGGESTED MAP *OS Explorer 260 Nottingham*

START/FINISH *Grid reference: SK 489313*

DOG FRIENDLINESS *Dogs can run free along the canal, but keep on lead when in nature reserve*

PARKING *Trent Lock car park*

PUBLIC TOILETS *At car park and Attenborough nature centre*

WALK 50 DIRECTIONS

Trent Lock lies where the River Soar flows into the Trent and where the Erewash Canal starts out on its way north towards the coalfields. It's a bright colourful place where East Midlands people come to see the boats. Sailing dinghies race by, while colourful barges take a more leisurely pace down the network of waterways. The Trent is a navigable hub here, with connections up the Soar to Leicester and beyond, west around the underside of the Pennines to the Mersey and east to the Humber and the North Sea, as well as the now shortened Erewash Canal which once penetrated the Peak District National Park to the north.

Turn right out of the car park and pass the Navigation Inn and its waterside garden to reach the banks of the River Trent. Turn left along the river bank, cross over the footbridge over the Erewash Canal by its confluence with the Trent. The Steamboat Inn and Lock House Tea Room will be on your left, and is usually busy with tourists.

Turn right along the Cranfleet Cut tow path. The Cut was built in 1798 so that the barges could avoid the river's Thrumpton Weir. At this point the eight huge cooling towers of the Ratcliffe power station dominate the scene.

Beyond two railway bridges carrying the busy Derby and Nottingham main lines, the Cut rejoins the Trent at Cranfleet Lock. The path now follows the river bank flood barriers. Ignore

WHILE YOU'RE THERE

Make sure you spend some time at Nottinghamshire Wildlife Trust's impressive new nature centre at Attenborough reserve. Apart from the café, shop and toilets, there are interactive displays and activities, plus a range of wildlife books and leaflets. The centre is open daily all year round.

WHERE TO EAT AND DRINK

The Navigation Inn at Trent Lock serves excellent bar meals in a large lounge bar with maps of various estuaries on the walls. The Steamboat Inn overlooks the locks themselves and serves equally good meals. Both inns are child friendly. For coffee and cream teas, try the Lock House Tea Room, while the airy, modern café at the Attenborough nature centre serves a range of snacks and light refreshments and boasts an outdoor terrace overlooking the wildlife-rich flooded gravel pits.

the circular walk waymarks and signs, and stick with the riverside. Past Thrumpton village on the far bank, the river meanders left and you see the first of many large artificial lakes.

You're now in the Attenborough Nature Reserve, a Site of Special Scientific Interest established in 1966. It extends across a series of disused gravel pits, which were excavated between 1929 and 1967. The pits show varying developments of natural vegetation. New plants colonise the reserve each year but you could well spot meadow saxifrage, flowering rush, ragged-robin and yellow rattle. Most eyes however will be focused on the abundant birdlife. This is an important wintering site for many wildfowl, including shoveler, mallard, wigeon and teal. In summer great crested grebe, shelduck, common tern and little ringed plover all come here to feed and breed, and you can often see a variety of warblers, including the rare grasshopper warbler.

Once again ignore a turn to the left, signed the Trent Valley Greenway, and follow the meanderings of the Trent by the gravel pits. Barton-in-Fabis, on the far bank of the river, shelters beneath a wooded hillside. The path passes a couple of secluded cottages, before crossing a footbridge over a waterway.

Just beyond the footbridge is a junction of tracks, by a nature reserve information board. Turn right and continue north along the bank, signposted 'Riverside Path to Beeston and Nottingham.'

Ignore the next two turnings on the left and when the boats of Beeston Marina come into sight on the river bend ahead turn left for a path away from the river signposted 'Meadow Lane'. This path goes between more pits before coming to the busy railway. The path turns left to follow the railway for 250yds (229m), then veers left again (south) through more woodland. Fork right at a junction and beyond a footbridge it enters suburban Attenborough.

Take the lane past the cricket ground, follow it round to the right, then turn left down Church Lane. Take the path signposted 'Barton Ferry Lane' through gates on the right of the churchyard, heading south between Ireton House and Poseidon House, back to the gravel pits. After 500yds (457m) emerge at the car park and nature centre (see box). Turn left over the bridge for a wide track back to meet the outward route by the riverside.

Walking in Safety

All these walks are suitable for any reasonably fit person, but less experienced walkers should try the easier walks first. Route finding is usually straightforward, but you will find that an Ordnance Survey map is a useful addition to the route maps and descriptions.

RISKS

Although each walk here has been researched with a view to minimising the risks to the walkers who follow its route, no walk in the countryside can be considered to be completely free from risk. Walking in the outdoors will always require a degree of common sense and judgement to ensure that it is as safe as possible.

- Be particularly careful on cliff paths and in upland terrain, where the consequences of a slip can be very serious.
- Remember to check tidal conditions before walking on the seashore.
- Some sections of route are by, or cross, busy roads. Take care and remember traffic is a danger even on minor country lanes.
- Be careful around farmyard machinery and livestock, especially if you have children with you.
- Be aware of the consequences of changes in the weather and check the forecast before you set out. Carry spare clothing and a torch if you are walking in the winter months. Remember the weather can change very quickly at any time of the year, and in moorland and heathland areas, mist and fog can make route finding much harder. Don't set out in these conditions unless you are confident of your navigation skills in poor visibility. In summer remember to take account of the heat and sun; wear a hat and carry spare water.
- On walks away from centres of population you should carry a whistle and survival bag. If you do have an accident requiring the emergency services, make a note of your position as accurately as possible and dial 999.

COUNTRYSIDE CODE

- Be safe, plan ahead and follow any signs.
- Leave gates and property as you find them.
- Protect plants and animals and take your litter home.
- Keep dogs under close control.
- Consider other people.

For more information visit www.countrysideaccess.gov.uk/things_to_know/countryside_code